# NATIONS
# OF THE WORLD
# MEXICO

*Jen Green*

www.raintreepublishers.co.uk
Visit our website to find out more information about Raintree books.

To order:
☎ Phone 44 (0) 1865 888113
🖹 Send a fax to 44 (0) 1865 314091
🖥 Visit the Raintree bookshop at www.raintreepublishers.co.uk to browse our catalogue and order online.

First published in Great Britain by Raintree, Halley Court, Jordan Hill, Oxford, OX2 8EJ, part of Harcourt Education Ltd.
Raintree is a registered trademark of Harcourt Education Ltd.

Produced for Raintree by the Brown Reference Group plc
Project Editor: Robert Anderson
Designer: Joan Curtis
Cartographers: Joan Curtis and William LeBihan
Picture Researcher: Brenda Clynch
Indexer: Kay Ollerenshaw

Raintree Publishers
Editors: Isabel Thomas and Kate Buckingham

Printed and bound in Singapore.

ISBN 1 844 21477 X
07 06 05 04 03
10 9 8 7 6 5 4 3 2 1

British Library cataloguing in publication data
Green, Jen
    Mexico – (Nations of the world)
    1. Human geography – Mexico – Juvenile literature
    2. Mexico – Geography – Juvenile literature
    I. Title
    917.2

A full catalogue is available for this book from the British Library.

Acknowledgements
*Front cover:* bullfighter waits his turn in the ring, Matamoros
*Title page: chacmool* at the temple of Chichén Itza

The acknowledgements on page 128 form part of this copyright page.

Every effort has been made to contact copyright holders of any material reproduced in this book. Any omissions will be rectified in subsequent printings if notice is given to the publishers.

# Contents

# Foreword

Since ancient times, people have gathered together in communities where they could share and trade resources and strive to build a safe and happy environment. Gradually, as populations grew and societies became more complex, communities expanded to become nations – groups of people who felt sufficiently bound by a common heritage to work together for a shared future.

Land has usually played an important role in defining a nation. People have a natural affection for the landscape in which they grew up. They are proud of its natural beauties – the mountains, rivers and forests – and of the towns and cities that flourish there. People are proud, too, of their nation's history – the shared struggles and achievements that have shaped the way they live today.

Religion, culture, race and lifestyle, too, have sometimes played a role in fostering a nation's identity. Often, though, a nation includes people of different races, beliefs and customs. Many have come from distant countries, and some want to preserve their traditional lifestyles.

Nations have rarely been fixed, unchanging things, either territorially or racially. Throughout history, borders have changed, often under the pressure of war, and people have migrated across the globe in search of a new life or of new land, or because they are fleeing from oppression or disaster. The world's nations are still changing today: some nations are breaking up and new nations are forming.

The modern nation of Mexico is the result of a meeting between two great civilizations: that of the ancient peoples of **Mesoamerica** and that of the Spanish empire that conquered the country in the 16th century. At first, the collision of these two civilizations was wholly disastrous. The Spanish killed and enslaved the native peoples and set out to destroy their cities, their art and their way of life. Over the years, however, the peoples have intermingled and learnt to live together. Today, Mexico's largely mixed-blood population can look back on almost two centuries of history as an independent nation.

# Introduction

Mexico is the southernmost country of North America, lying on a horn-shaped slice of land between the Atlantic and Pacific oceans. To the north, Mexico borders the USA; to the south are the Central American countries of Guatemala and Belize.

Mexico is a land of many contrasts. There are sandy beaches fringed with palm trees and deserts dotted with cacti; vast, bustling cities and sleepy ancient towns; old whitewashed churches as well as shiny, modern sky-scrapers. Mexico has one of the fastest-growing economies in the world, and yet it is also a country that holds on to its traditions. This is a land of simple farms and high-tech industries where people may just as easily travel by ox cart as catch a plane.

Mexico's striking contrasts reflect its mixed origins. The modern country is the result of a marriage between two peoples – the native Indians and the colonial Spanish – and their cultures. Before the 16th century, advanced civilizations, such as those of the **Aztecs** and **Maya**, flourished in Mexico. Although the arrival of the Spanish in 1519 brought about the destruction of many ancient cities and their peoples, the Indians and their way of life had a lasting impact on the new country. Over the years, the Spanish and Indian communities have mingled, and their separate traditions merged to create the lively, colourful Mexican culture of today.

*Most country towns in Mexico feature a main square, called the zócalo, where the market is held. It is usually the site of the town's church, too.*

## FACT FILE

● Mexico's name comes from the word by which the most famous and most powerful of its ancient peoples, the Aztecs, called themselves: *Mexica* (pronounced *mesh-EE-ca*).

● The major ethnic division in Mexico is between those of mixed Spanish and Indian blood (called **mestizos**) and native peoples (**indígenas**, or Indians).

● Mexico, together with the nations of Central and South America, is part of Latin America. 'Latin' refers to the Latin-derived languages – either Spanish or Portuguese – that most of the people of these nations speak.

There are four denominations of Mexican bank notes in circulation: the 10, 20, 50 and 100 nuevo peso notes. Each shows a famous personality from Mexican history. The N$100 note shows Cuauhtémoc, the last Aztec emperor, while the N$20 note shows the 19th-century Mexican president Benito Juárez.

## NAME, MONEY AND FLAG

The official name of Mexico is the United States of Mexico (*Estados Unidos Mexicanos*), but most Mexicans refer to their country simply as *la Republica* – the Republic. They use Mexico – *México* – to refer to the capital city. In the English-speaking world, however, this is generally called Mexico City in order to distinguish it from the country of Mexico.

Mexico's currency is the Mexican new peso (nuevo peso), which is usually written N$. There are 100 centavos – written ¢ – to the peso. A price is sometimes written as, say, $75mn, where 'mn' is short for *moneda nacional* (national money). This distinguishes it from the US dollar, which many shops accept as payment.

The Mexican flag has vertical bands of green, white and red. The green stands for independence, the white for the Roman Catholic religion and the red for the unity of the people. In the centre is Mexico's coat of arms, which shows an eagle perched on a cactus with a snake in its beak. According to Aztec legend, the gods told the Aztec people that they would build a great city where they saw an eagle feeding in this way. This city was Tenochtitlán, the ancient site that lies buried beneath the modern capital, Mexico City.

After Mexico won its independence from Spain in 1821, the government chose a tricolour – three stripes – as the country's national flag.

WHERE DOES MEXICO'S POPULATION LIVE?

75%
cities and towns

25%
countryside

*The vast majority of people live in Mexico's cities and towns.*

## LANGUAGE AND PEOPLE

The official language of Mexico is Spanish (see page 102). This dates back to the 300-year period when the country was ruled by Spain. Today, almost all Mexicans speak Castilian Spanish, although it has a softer sound than the version spoken in Spain. Some 5 million people speak one or more of the 50 or so Indian languages, such as **Náhuatl**, Maya and Huastec – some

## Pronouncing Spanish and pre-Hispanic names

Pronouncing Mexican Spanish words and names is not difficult. Most letters are pronounced just as they are in English. There are a few exceptions, however:

c   pronounced like *s* when before e or i; otherwise it is pronounced like *k*

g   pronounced like *h* before e or i; otherwise it is pronounced like *g* in go

gu   pronounced like *g* in go

h   not pronounced (silent)

j   pronounced like a rough *h*

ll   pronounced like *y*

ñ   pronounced like *ny* in 'canyon'

qu   pronounced like *k*

r   is rolled

v   pronounced like *b*

x   pronounced like *h* after e or i and otherwise like *x* in 'taxi'. In words taken from Indian languages, *x* is pronounced *sh*

z   always pronounced like *s*

Usually in Spanish, words are stressed on the last syllable. If, however, a word is written with an accent, the syllable containing the accent is usually stressed instead. Pre-Hispanic names – that is, the names of people and places of Mexico's ancient civilizations – are usually spelt and pronounced as if they were Spanish.

Try pronouncing some of the names in this book: México (*MEH-hee-ko*), Cortés (*cor-TESS*), Quetzalcóatl (*ket-sal-CO-atl*), Estados Unidos (*es-TA-dos oo-NEE-dos*) and Tenochtitlán (*te-noch-tee-TLAN*).

# POPULATION DENSITY

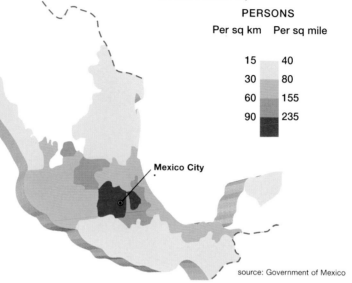

The population of Mexico is very unevenly distributed. The vast majority of people live in the cities of the central highland region, around Mexico City.

**PERSONS**

| Per sq km | | Per sq mile |
|---|---|---|
| 15 | | 40 |
| 30 | | 80 |
| 60 | | 155 |
| 90 | | 235 |

Mexico City

source: Government of Mexico

*Below and opposite:*
*In the 20th century,*
*improved health care*
*brought about a rapid*
*rise in Mexico's*
*population. This trend*
*has created a very*
*young population.*

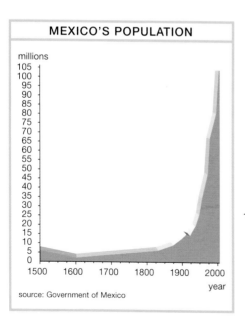

**MEXICO'S POPULATION**

millions

source: Government of Mexico

of the languages of Mexico's original inhabitants. Many native words have passed into Mexican Spanish, too.

The vast majority of Mexican people are *mestizo*, which means that they are of 'mixed' Indian and Spanish blood. There are some full-blooded Indians, most of whom live in separate communities in Mexico's rural areas. There is a small minority of people descended from slaves brought from Africa.

Mexico has a population of 97.4 million people. It is one of the fastest-growing nations in the world. Experts estimate that by the year 2015, the population will top 119 million. This demographic explosion has created economic and social problems, since the government is unable to provide enough jobs or welfare for everyone.

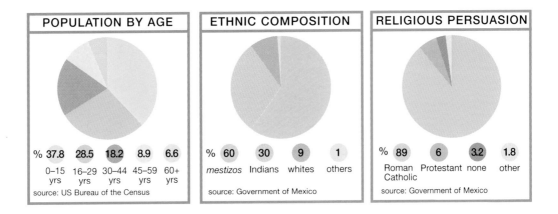

| POPULATION BY AGE | | | | |
|---|---|---|---|---|
| % 37.8 | 28.5 | 18.2 | 8.9 | 6.6 |
| 0–15 yrs | 16–29 yrs | 30–44 yrs | 45–59 yrs | 60+ yrs |

source: US Bureau of the Census

| ETHNIC COMPOSITION | | | |
|---|---|---|---|
| % 60 | 30 | 9 | 1 |
| *mestizos* | Indians | whites | others |

source: Government of Mexico

| RELIGIOUS PERSUASION | | | |
|---|---|---|---|
| % 89 | 6 | 3.2 | 1.8 |
| Roman Catholic | Protestant | none | other |

source: Government of Mexico

The average population density is about 49 people per square kilometre (127 per square mile), but Mexico's population is not evenly spread. In both area and population, the capital, Mexico City (see pages 28–36), is one of the largest cities in the world. Three-quarters of Mexicans live in urban areas – which take up a relatively small part of the land – leaving only a quarter of the population living in the countryside.

In the 20th century, millions of people left the poorer rural areas to find work in the cities. Millions, too, have migrated to the USA, often crossing the US–Mexican border illegally (see pages 21 and 68). Once in the USA, the Mexican immigrants' lack of legal status makes them vulnerable to poor working conditions.

Mexico has no official religion, but the vast majority (89 per cent) of people are Roman Catholic. There are also some Protestants and Jews, as well as Indians who follow their ancient religious traditions, sometimes alongside Christian beliefs (see page 113).

# The national anthem

In the mid-19th century, the government of the newly independent Mexico chose a rousing poem by the Mexican poet Francisco González Bocanegra (1824–1908) as the words for the country's national anthem. Here is a translation:

*Mexicans, at the cry of war*
*Make ready your sword and horse,*
*Let the core of your land resound*
*To the sonorous roar of the cannon.*
*Fatherland! Be crowned with*
*the olive branch*
*Of peace by the divine archangel,*
*For in heaven your eternal destiny*
*Was written by the finger of God.*

*But if a foreign enemy dares*
*To profane your land with his foot,*
*Remember, dear Fatherland,*
*that Heaven*
*Has given you a soldier in*
*each son.*

# Land and cities

*'And when we saw all those cities and villages built in the water, and other great towns on dry land ... we were amazed.'*

Bernal Díaz del Castillo, historian of the Spanish conquest of Mexico

Mexico forms a huge, wedge-shaped bridge of land between the USA and Central America. The wedge is broadest in the north, where Mexico shares a border of 2993 kilometres (1860 miles) with the USA. From here, the country curves south and east towards Central America like a giant sickle. It tapers as it curves, and its narrowest point is only 225 kilometres (140 miles) wide. Mexico shares its southern borders with the countries of Guatemala and Belize.

Straddling the Tropic of Cancer, Mexico covers a total area of 1,972,545 square kilometres (761,600 square miles) and is the 14th-largest country in the world. It is about one-quarter the size of Australia and slightly less than four times the size of Spain.

To the west and east, Mexico is bounded by great oceans. The Pacific Ocean lies to the west, and to the east is the Gulf of Mexico and the Caribbean Sea, which are part of the Atlantic Ocean. Mexico has about 9380 kilometres (5830 miles) of coastline.

In the north-west is Baja California (Lower California), a long finger of extremely arid land that stretches 1220 kilometres (758 miles) into the Pacific and is separated from the mainland by the Gulf of California. It is the longest peninsula in the world. In the far south-east is the Yucatán Peninsula, a lopsided square of land that juts into the Gulf of Mexico.

*The deserts that cover much of northern Mexico sometimes bloom with dense, colourful vegetation, such as the barrel cactus and the pink cliff-rose.*

FACT FILE

- The lowest point in Mexico's inland is Lake Salada at 10 m (33 ft) above sea level. The highest is Mount Orizaba at 5699 m (18,696 ft).

- Mexico has few major rivers or natural lakes. The longest river is the Río Bravo del Norte (called the Rio Grande in the USA), which flows for 3025 km (1880 miles) and forms the border with the USA.

- Geologically, Mexico lies on the western edge of the huge North American Plate. It is one of the most unstable regions of the Earth and is prone to both volcanic activity and earthquakes.

## MEXICO'S TERRAIN

Legend has it that when Mexico's Spanish conqueror, Hernán Cortés (1485–1547), was asked to describe the country, he crumpled up a piece of paper and tossed it onto a table in order to demonstrate the wrinkled, mountainous lie of the land. Mexico certainly has plenty of mountains: mountain ranges or high tableland cover more than two-thirds of the country.

*Mexico's Barranca del Cobre (Copper Canyon) is as deep as the Grand Canyon in the USA and four times as large, although its scenery is not quite as dramatic.*

### A land of mountains

There are three great ranges of mountains, forming the Sierra Madre **cordillera**. Two of the ranges run almost the length of the country, parallel to the east and west coasts. These are the Sierra Madre Oriental and the Sierra Madre Occidental. In the south, a third range – the Sierra Madre del Sur – runs south-eastwards through the states of Guerrero and Oaxaca. These three ranges enclose a great highland region called the Mexican Plateau.

The Sierra Madre Oriental stretches from the barren hills of the Río Bravo del Norte southwards through the states of Coahuila, Nuevo León, Querétaro, Hidalgo, Tlaxcala and Puebla. The range creates a dramatic, wild landscape of caves and canyons, waterfalls and lakes, together with rich deposits of coal and iron. In the north-eastern foothills of the range lies the modern industrial city of Monterrey (see pages 39–40).

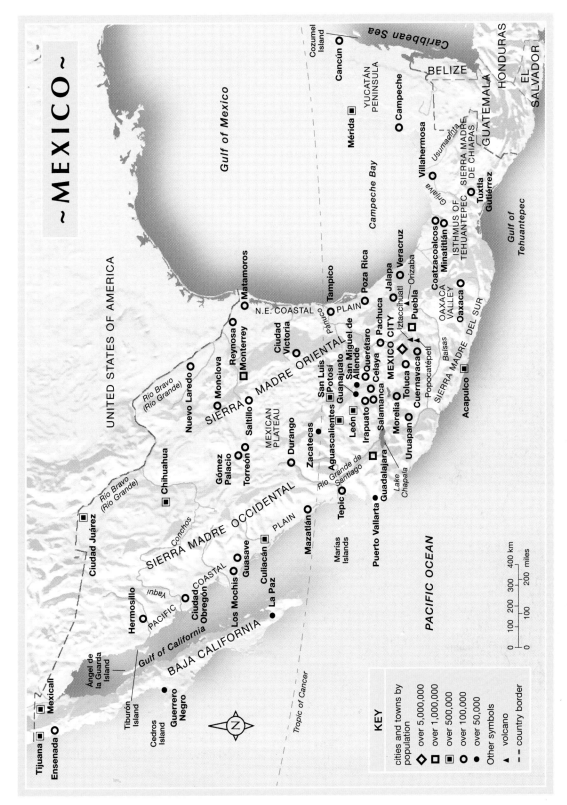

~MEXICO~

Caribbean Sea

HONDURAS

EL SALVADOR

GUATEMALA

BELIZE

Cozumel Island

Cancún

YUCATÁN PENINSULA

Mérida

Campeche

Gulf of Mexico

Campeche Bay

Villahermosa

SIERRA MADRE DE CHIAPAS

Usumacinta

Grijalva

Tuxtla Gutiérrez

ISTHMUS OF TEHUANTEPEC

Gulf of Tehuantepec

Coatzacoalcos

Minatitlán

Veracruz

Orizaba

OAXACA VALLEY

Oaxaca

SIERRA MADRE DEL SUR

Poza Rica

Jalapa

Pachuca

Iztaccíhuatl

Puebla

Popocatépetl

Tampico

Pánuco

N.E. COASTAL PLAIN

PLAIN

Matamoros

Reynosa

Monterrey

Ciudad Victoria

SIERRA MADRE ORIENTAL

UNITED STATES OF AMERICA

Río Bravo (Río Grande)

Nuevo Laredo

Monclova

Saltillo

MEXICAN PLATEAU

San Luis Potosí

San Miguel de Allende

Guanajuato

Querétaro

Celaya

MEXICO CITY

Toluca

Cuernavaca

Salamanca

León

Irapuato

Morelia

Uruapan

Balsas

Acapulco

Durango

Zacatecas

Aguascalientes

Río Grande de Santiago

Guadalajara

Lake Chapala

Tepic

Gómez Palacio

Torreón

Chihuahua

Conchos

Río Bravo (Río Grande)

Ciudad Juárez

SIERRA MADRE OCCIDENTAL

PLAIN

Mazatlán

Marías Islands

Puerto Vallarta

PACIFIC OCEAN

COASTAL

PACIFIC

Hermosillo

Yaqui

Ciudad Obregón

Los Mochis

Guasave

Culiacán

La Paz

Gulf of California

BAJA CALIFORNIA

Ángel de la Guarda Island

Tiburón Island

Cedros Island

Guerrero Negro

Tropic of Cancer

Tijuana

Mexicali

Ensenada

N

0 100 200 300 400 km
0 100 200 miles

KEY

cities and towns by population

◇ over 5,000,000
□ over 1,000,000
■ over 500,000
○ over 100,000
● over 50,000

Other symbols

▲ volcano
-- country border

15

*The wild, dramatic landscape of the Sierra Madre Occidental is typically covered by grass and scrub. The remoteness of this mountainous region long made it a refuge for various Indian peoples who wanted to escape Spanish rule.*

The Sierra Madre Occidental is steeper and more rugged than the eastern range. It rises from close to the US border and gradually gathers height as it passes southwards through the states of Chihuahua and Durango. Its sheer western side is cut by deep canyons called *barrancas*, some of which are 1500 metres (5000 feet) deep. The most spectacular of these is the Barranca del Cobre (Copper Canyon).

The Sierra Madre del Sur extends from the Sierra Madre Occidental into the southern Mexican states of Guerrero and Oaxaca and as far as the Isthmus of Tehuantepec. This range is cut by deep ravines, making the surrounding region relatively inaccessible and a haven for traditional Indian cultures. Along the coast, the mountains fall steeply to the sea, and there are some fine natural harbours, including the tourist resort of Acapulco.

# THE DISTRICT AND STATES OF MEXICO

Mexico is composed of 31 states and the Federal District. These areas vary widely in size and character, from the vast and thinly populated desert states of the north-west, such as Chihuahua and Sonora, to the tiny, largely urban Federal District and the poor and largely rural Indian-dominated states of the south, such as Chiapas and Oaxaca. This map shows both the states and the state capitals (•).

From the Isthmus of Tehuantepec to the border with Guatemala is the Sierra Madre de Chiapas, which completes Mexico's spine of mountains. Cocoa has been grown on the range's lower slopes since **Aztec** times.

## A zone of volcanoes

A range of volcanoes, called the Cordillera Neo-Volcánica, runs across the country south of the capital, Mexico City. It contains many high volcanic peaks, including Mount Orizaba, also known as Citlaltépetl. At 5699 metres (18,696 feet), it is the highest mountain in Mexico.

Two of Mexico's most famous volcanoes are Popocatépetl, the name of which means 'smoking mountain', and Iztaccíhuatl, which means 'sleeping woman'. Seen from Mexico City, they are usually swathed in smog, but they form a dramatic backdrop to the nearby city of Puebla. Aztec legend tells that the mountains were built by Popo, a mighty warrior who was in love with Ixta, a

1 BAJA CALIFORNIA NORTE
Mexicali

2 BAJA CALIFORNIA SUR
La Paz

3 SONORA
Hermosillo

4 CHIHUAHUA
Chihuahua

5 SINALOA
Culiacán

6 DURANGO
Durango

7 COAHUILA
Saltillo

8 NUEVO LEÓN
Monterrey

9 ZACATECAS
Zacatecas

10 NAYARIT
Tepic

11 JALISCO
Guadalajara

12 AGUASCALIENTES
Aguascalientes

13 SAN LUIS POTOSÍ
San Luis Potosí

14 TAMAULIPAS
Ciudad Victoria

15 COLIMA
Colima

16 GUANAJUATO
Guanajuato

17 QUERÉTARO
Querétaro

18 MICHOACÁN
Morelia

19 HIDALGO
Pachuca

20 ESTADO DE MÉXICO
Toluca

21 FEDERAL DISTRICT
Mexico City

22 MORELOS
Cuernavaca

23 TLAXCALA
Tlaxcala

24 PUEBLA
Puebla

25 GUERRERO
Chilpancingo

26 OAXACA
Oaxaca

27 VERACRUZ
Jalapa

28 TABASCO
Villahermosa

29 CHIAPAS
Tuxtla Gutiérrez

30 CAMPECHE
Campeche

31 YUCATÁN
Mérida

32 QUINTANA ROO
Chetumal

## Mexico's volcanoes

A volcano is a mountain formed by an eruption of gas and hot, liquid rock called lava from deep inside the Earth. When a volcano erupts, lava is forced to the surface and gradually forms a mountain. Hot gas and ash are hurled high into the air.

Volcanic eruptions are linked to movements in the Earth's rocky outer crust. This crust is made up of sections called tectonic plates, which fit together like a jigsaw puzzle. Where plates clash together, as they do off the west coast of Mexico, one plate dives below the other. The resulting friction causes the rocks to melt and expand. The liquid rock rises to the surface to form a volcano. Movements of the Earth's crust can also trigger earthquakes.

Mexico's youngest volcano, Paricutín, was formed in 1943. That year, a farmer in western Mexico noticed a small, smoking pit in his cornfield. The following day he found that it had grown into a cone 6 m (20 ft) high. Paricutín erupted for the next nine years, gradually burying eleven villages and hamlets. Today, the volcano is a mountain 2807 m (9210 ft) tall.

Another volcano, Mount Chichonal in the Chiapas Highlands, erupted in 1982 but proved far more destructive. Lava-flows from the volcano buried villages and killed 3500 people.

Two of Mexico's most famous volcanoes, Popocatépetl and Iztaccíhuatl, which lie close to Mexico City and Puebla, are pictured above.

beautiful princess. After Ixta died while Popo was away fighting, the returning hero laid her body on top of Iztaccíhuatl. Then he stood guard on Popocatépetl, holding a smoking torch.

Both peaks are more than 5000 metres (16,400 feet) high. Today, Ixtaccíhuatl is classified as dormant – that is, no longer active. Popocatépetl, however, is showing signs of renewed volcanic activity. In 1994, ash from its explosions covered the city of Puebla with dust. Experts are worried that Popocatépetl may soon have a major eruption. The lives of the people who live on the flanks of the volcano would be threatened, and ash from an eruption could endanger aircraft using Mexico City's international airport.

**There have been some 30 recorded eruptions of Popocatépetl. Most of these eruptions were restricted to steam and ash emission.**

## Where are Mexico's volcanoes?

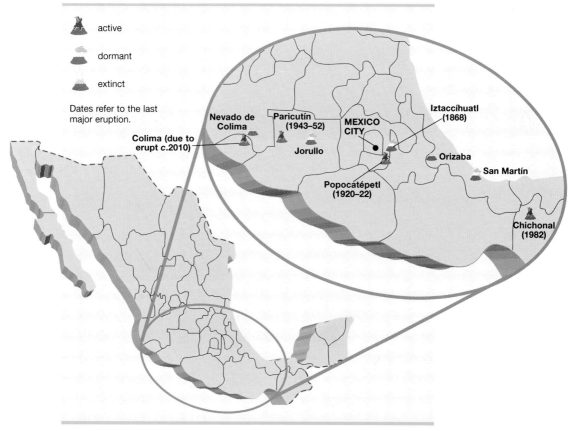

active

dormant

extinct

Dates refer to the last major eruption.

Nevado de Colima

Colima (due to erupt c.2010)

Paricutín (1943–52)

Jorullo

MEXICO CITY

Popocatépetl (1920–22)

Iztaccíhuatl (1868)

Orizaba

San Martín

Chichonal (1982)

### The Mexican Plateau

The eastern and western Sierra Madre mountains and the volcanic chain form a great U-shaped ridge of high ground that encloses a vast plateau in the centre of Mexico. The plateau is in two parts. In the north, towards the US border, is the lower and drier Mesa del Norte. In the south is the Mesa Central, or Altiplano, which is both wetter and higher, rising to about 2100 metres (6900 feet). Broad, fertile valleys separated by volcanic peaks cut through the plateau.

This southern section of the Mexican Plateau has long formed the heartland of Mexico and is the country's most densely populated area. Many of Mexico's greatest cities, including Mexico City and the large cities of Guadalajara and Puebla, have grown up in the broad valleys in the Altiplano.

*Much of the landscape of the north and the west of Mexico is desert. The tall, spindly plant is a boojum tree, which grows only in the Mexican states of Baja California and Sonora. The boojum tree can grow up to 15 metres (50 feet) tall.*

## The north-west

The north-west of Mexico is mainly desert – a dry, barren land dotted with cacti. In some years, no rain falls at all, and farming is possible only near rivers and oases watered by underground springs.

In the far west, the peninsula of Baja (Lower) California, with its rocky spine of mountains, is mostly arid. For a long time, it was one of Mexico's wildest and most inaccessible regions. At its northern end, close to the US border, are the tourist towns of Tijuana and Mexicali. These are popular destinations for daytrippers from the USA. During the Prohibition period in the USA (1920–33), drinkers came to the resorts to escape the anti-alcohol laws. Today, many people come to place bets on the greyhound races, bullfights and **jai alai** matches (see page 112) that take place there.

Most people, however, venture further south along the peninsula to enjoy the wide range of activities and sports available along its largely unspoilt coasts, including fishing, windsurfing and snorkelling. Experts estimate that the Gulf of California is home to some 800 species of fish as well as many kinds of whales. In spring, people flock to Scammon's Lagoon (see pages 25 and 26) to watch hundreds of whales gathering offshore to breed.

## The coastal plains

In a country with so many mountains, Mexico's coastal strips are rare and precious areas of flat, low-lying land. Parts of the coastal lowlands make good farming country. Along the west coast, the lowland strip is narrow, but where river valleys cut inland, the soil is very fertile.

## The Line

Mexicans call the border with the USA '**la Linea**' – the Line. Going into Mexico from the USA is usually very easy. Tourists from the USA visiting Mexican border towns such as Tijuana and towns a little further south such as Ensenada and San Felipe do not even have to go through passport or customs checks. For people crossing the Line northwards, however, border controls are much stricter. This is because of concerns in the USA about illegal immigration.

'In general, California is disagreeable and horrid … its land broken and arid, exceedingly stony and sandy; and lacking in water; if two or three showers fall in a year the Californians count themselves lucky.' An 18th-century visitor to Baja California

In the east, the strip bordering the Gulf of Mexico is much wider. In the north, this area is dry and covered by thorny scrub. Towards the south, rainfall increases, and much of the middle section is swamp land, with some lagoons. The southern end of the strip is covered by dense rainforest and is home to tropical birds and animals, such as parrots and monkeys.

*Cozumel Island lies about 20 kilometres (12 miles) off the east coast of the Yucatán Peninsula. In the language of the local Mayan people, the island's name means 'island of swallows'. Its beautiful coral reefs make it popular with divers and snorkellers.*

## The Yucatán Peninsula

In the far south-east of Mexico, the Yucatán Peninsula is a large, low-lying plateau made of limestone. Limestone is a soft rock that is permeable (water seeps through it). In the Yucatán, some rivers run in underground channels, and in places the water has worn away large underground caverns. Sometimes the cavern roofs collapse, leaving natural wells called ***cenotes***.

Along the coastline, fine beaches edged with palm trees alternate with mangrove swamps. Cancún is a famous tourist resort (see page 86). Off the east coast, the large island of Cozumel is renowned for its coral reefs.

## MEXICO'S CLIMATE

Mexico's Spanish conquerors divided the country into three climate zones based on height. These divisions still hold true today. The lowest zone, from sea level to 790 metres (2600 feet), is called the *tierra caliente* (hot land). This zone has long, hot summers and mild winters. The middle zone, up to about 1700 metres (5580 feet), is called the *tierra templada* (temperate land). This area enjoys a mild climate with temperatures between 10 and 27 °C (50 and 80 °F). Most of Mexico's people live within this zone. Above 1700 metres (5580 feet) lies the *tierra fría* (cold land). Temperatures here can be very cold at night.

In the deserts of northern Mexico, few clouds gather to shield the land from the searing heat of the sun or to keep the warmth in at night. As with most deserts, this area is extremely hot by day and bitterly cold at night.

Much of Mexico is dry, and rain is eagerly awaited. More rain falls in the tropical south than in the north. The land in northern Mexico is arid because it lies in the so-called horse latitudes – belts of calm air where few rain clouds form. Further south, mountains near the Atlantic and Pacific coasts receive heavy rainfall, particularly on slopes facing wet, sea-borne winds. Less rain falls inland and on sheltered mountain slopes.

Some parts of eastern and southern Mexico experience the opposite problem to that of the north – too much rain falls. Wild plants grow so well that farmers have to hack down growth to plant their crops. The rainforests in the far south have a long rainy season in summer, when showers fall every afternoon.

*The capital, Mexico City, and the port of Veracruz are only some 430 kilometres (270 miles) apart. Nevertheless, they have very different climates. Veracruz, which lies on the Gulf Coast, is hot and humid all year round, with a wet summer. By contrast, Mexico City, which lies inland and at a much higher elevation, has a milder, more temperate climate.*

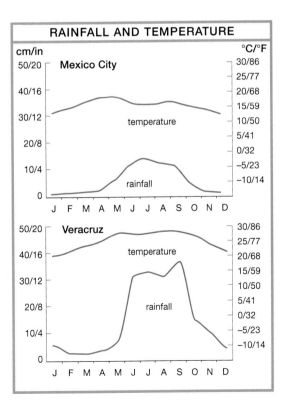

**RAINFALL AND TEMPERATURE**

Mexico City

Veracruz

## WILDLIFE AND PLANTS

Mexico's wildlife is as varied as its scenery. Different kinds of plants and animals live in the country's deserts, mountains, plains and rainforests.

*This cactus serves as both home and food to the gila woodpecker. Here the woodpecker drinks nectar from the flowers of a cactus.*

### The flowering desert

The deserts are home to many varieties of cacti, including prickly pear and **saguaro**, a giant cactus that can grow up to 15 metres (50 feet) tall. **Agaves** are also desert-loving plants, with a base of spiny leaves and a tall, spectacular head of flowers.

Mexicans put the agave to an astonishing variety of uses. The agave called **henequen** produces a tough fibre that Mexicans use to make rope and cloth. The sap of another agave, the **maguey**, is used to make tequila, the famous Mexican liquor. Some agave flowers are edible and are cooked in tortillas (see page 107).

The plants and animals of Mexico's deserts are able to survive high daytime temperatures and the lack of water. The gila woodpecker and the cactus wren both make their nests in spiny cactus plants, which also provide them with nectar to drink. Desert-loving reptiles include iguanas, deadly rattlesnakes, tortoises and large, poisonous lizards called gila monsters.

Mammals include coyotes and prairie dogs. The world's smallest dog, the chihuahua, originally came from Mexico and is named after the northern desert state of Chihuahua. Experts believe that the chihuahua is the descendant of the *techichi*, a small, barkless dog kept by the ancient **Toltec** people.

## Whales and butterflies

On the west coast of Baja California is a clear, shallow bay called Laguna Ojo de Liebre, or Scammon's Lagoon, close to Guerrero Negro. Grey whales make the 9700-kilometre (6000-mile) journey from the Arctic to the warm waters there to give birth to their young. They stay only for a short while, from early January to early March, before they return north. During this period, tourists can take boat trips on whale-watching excursions. Sometimes they even get the chance to touch the whales.

Another famous visitor to Mexico is the monarch butterfly. These striking orange-and-black insects migrate from the northern USA and Canada to valleys in the state of Michoacán, in south-western Mexico. They arrive in huge groups in autumn and spend the winter resting in clusters on tree trunks. In spring, the butterflies fly north again.

*Each year, between 30 and 100 million monarch butterflies migrate to the forested mountains of Michoacán. They rest on tree trunks, sometimes covering the trunks entirely.*

## The threatened green turtle

Scammon's Lagoon is one of the few remaining nesting sites in the world of the green turtle. For centuries, large numbers of these reptiles have grazed in the warm waters of the tropics. The turtles were highly prized by native peoples who lived on the coast, for whom turtle meat and eggs were an important source of food.

After the Europeans reached the Americas in the early 16th century, they netted the turtles in vast numbers. Turtle soup was a great delicacy in European cities, and from the 19th century, turtle meat was widely sold in tins. The green turtle became very rare, and in the 1970s, it was placed on the official list of the world's threatened species and netting it was banned. More recently, the Mexican government has launched a protection programme for egg-laying turtles.

### In the thick of the forest

Great forests grow on the highland slopes of Mexico. Trees include valuable hardwoods such as mahogany and rosewood. Pine, a fast-growing softwood, is also prized as timber. On the higher, remote slopes are black bears, mountain lions, deer and bighorn sheep.

In Mexico's far south and east, lush, tropical rainforest covers parts of the land. Trees are festooned with vines and colourful orchids. Jungle birds include humming-birds, parrots and the **queztal**. This bird has brilliant blue and green feathers, and the male of the species has the longest tail feathers of any bird. The ancient peoples of **Mesoamerica** used the feathers for decoration, ceremonial clothing and battle dress. During the conquest, Spanish warriors were terrified when they saw the Aztec warriors completely covered in queztal plumes. They looked, the Spanish are reputed to have said, 'as if a volcano had burst'. Today, the quetzal's habitat is under threat and the bird is very rare.

There are some 250 threatened animal species in Mexico. These include the jaguar, the Cozumel Island coati and the Veracruz quail-dove.

*A jaguar pauses at the water's edge. The jaguar is the largest cat in the Americas. It is found from the US–Mexico border south to Argentina, although its survival is now threatened in Mexico. The ancient Aztec people admired the jaguar and named a military order after this great hunter.*

## MEXICO'S CITIES

*The twin volcanoes of Popocatépetl and Iztaccíhuatl used to be an everyday feature of Mexico City's skyline. Today, though, the volcanoes are usually hidden behind the thick city smog. It is only on clear and breezy days that the volcanoes spectacularly reappear.*

Almost three-quarters of Mexico's inhabitants live in cities or in the sprawling suburbs and satellite towns that usually surround them. Such urban spaces are lively and vibrant, but they are often overcrowded and badly polluted. Extremes of wealth and poverty exist side by side (see pages 104–5).

### Mexico City

Mexico City, like the country of which it is the capital, is full of contradictions. One minute, it is alive with colour and movement; the next minute, it is grey and dreary. Within Mexico City there are dazzling wealth and miserable poverty, vast parks and smog-laden air, splendid museums and sprawling slums. Mexico City is home to the national government and is the industrial and business capital of Mexico.

The most striking thing about the Mexican capital is its size. The Federal District of Mexico is five times the size of the next biggest town, Guadalajara, spreading out over some 1100 square kilometres (425 square miles). With about 18 million inhabitants, it is the second-largest city in the world, a ranking it shares with Bombay in India. Each week, thousands of people arrive in search of work,

*Mexicans call their capital simply México or 'el DF' (el day-efay), standing for Distrito Federal (Federal District).*

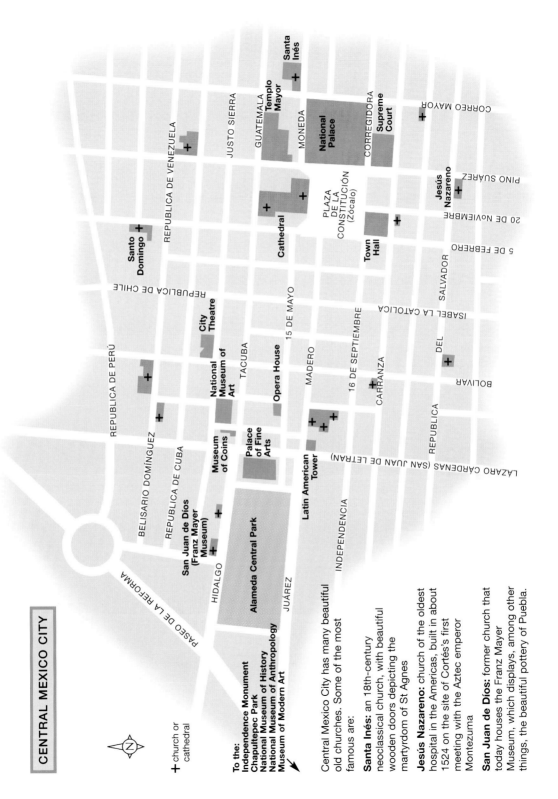

## CENTRAL MEXICO CITY

+ church or
cathedral

**To the:**
Independence Monument
Chapultepec Park
National Museum of History
National Museum of Anthropology
Museum of Modern Art

Central Mexico City has many beautiful old churches. Some of the most famous are:

**Santa Inés:** an 18th-century neoclassical church, with beautiful wooden doors depicting the martyrdom of St Agnes

**Jesús Nazareno:** church of the oldest hospital in the Americas, built in about 1524 on the site of Cortés's first meeting with the Aztec emperor Montezuma

**San Juan de Dios:** former church that today houses the Franz Mayer Museum, which displays, among other things, the beautiful pottery of Puebla.

Map labels:

PASEO DE LA REFORMA
HIDALGO
JUÁREZ
San Juan de Dios (Franz Mayer Museum)
Alameda Central Park
BELISARIO DOMÍNGUEZ
REPUBLICA DE CUBA
Museum of Coins
Palace of Fine Arts
REPUBLICA DE PERÚ
National Museum of Art
City Theatre
REPUBLICA DE CHILE
Santo Domingo
REPUBLICA DE VENEZUELA
JUSTO SIERRA
GUATEMALA
Templo Mayor
Santa Inés
MONEDA
National Palace
CORREGIDORA
Supreme Court
CORREO MAYOR
PINO SUÁREZ
Jesús Nazareno
20 DE NOVIEMBRE
5 DE FEBRERO
SALVADOR
ISABEL LA CATOLICA
DEL
BOLIVAR
CARRANZA
16 DE SEPTIEMBRE
REPUBLICA
LAZARO CARDENAS (SAN JUAN DE LETRAN)
INDEPENDENCIA
Latin American Tower
MADERO
TACUBA
Opera House
15 DE MAYO
Cathedral
PLAZA DE LA CONSTITUCIÓN (Zócalo)
Town Hall

29

**The inhabitants of Mexico's capital city are called *capitalinos* or, more popularly, *chilangos*.**

and many set up home in illegal shanty towns called *ciudades perdidas* (lost cities). Mexico City is still growing fast, and its polluted urban sprawl has spread way beyond the official borders of the Federal District.

The city lies in the high, fertile Valley of Mexico, surrounded by snow-covered mountains. At an altitude of 2240 metres (7350 feet), the climate is pleasant, and at one time, the city was famous for its clean air. Today, though, the air is heavily polluted by factory and car fumes. The mountains and warm air currents trap the pollution within the valley, causing breathing difficulties and sore eyes for inhabitants and visitors alike.

Mexico City stands on the site of Tenochtitlán, the ancient capital of the Aztec empire. The Aztec city stood on an island in the middle of Lake Texcoco and was connected to the mainland by three causeways. It was a patchwork of canals, gardens and red pyramid-temples.

When the Spanish arrived there in 1519, they were amazed by its size and beauty. One of the Spaniards, Bernal Díaz del Castello, later wrote about their first sight of Lake Texcoco and its settlements. The soldiers, he wrote, could hardly believe their eyes: 'And when we saw all those cities and villages built in the water, and

*The huge main square of Mexico City, the Zócalo, measures some 240 by 240 metres (787 by 787 feet). On the left of the picture is the cathedral, and on the right, the Palacio Nacional.*

# MEXICO CITY METRO

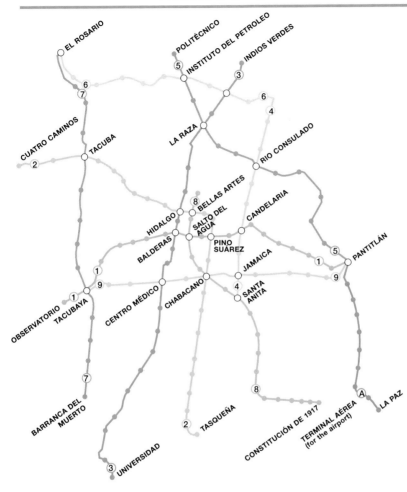

**KEY**

| | |
|---|---|
| ① | line number |
| ●— | station |
| ○ | interchange station |

The best way to get around in Mexico City is by the metro (the underground rail network). It is very modern and efficient, although it can get very crowded and hot in rush hour. There are currently ten lines, although new lines and stations are being planned.

other great towns on dry land, and that straight and level causeway leading to Mexico, we were astounded. These great towns ... rising from the water, all made of stone, seemed like an enchanted vision ... Indeed some of our soldiers asked whether it was not all a dream.'

The Spaniards' admiration did not, however, stop them from demolishing the city. In its place, they built a new city as the capital of the colony they named New Spain. It was European in style, with broad avenues, elegant squares and imposing buildings. It was built out of local materials, such as the red volcanic rock called *tezontle*, which the Aztecs had used to build their temples.

**The Spanish based the new city on a grid plan, still visible today. The Indians were confined to the city outskirts.**

Despite flooding and earthquake damage, this early Spanish city remains at the core of present-day Mexico City. In the 19th century, much of Lake Texcoco was drained, and the city spread across the valley.

At the heart of the city is the **Zócalo**, a vast square that stands on the site of the most important Aztec temples. Now officially called the Plaza de la Constitución, it is the second-largest public square in the world after Moscow's Red Square.

On the east side of the Zócalo is the 18th-century Palacio Nacional (National Palace), which houses the offices of the federal president. This impressive building stands on the site of the 16th-century Aztec palace of emperor Montezuma II. Around the building's courtyard are murals (wall paintings) by the famous artist Diego Rivera (see pages 95 and 97). The murals tell the history of Mexico from the time of the Aztecs to the 1910 revolution (see pages 64–6) and beyond.

On the north side of the square is the cathedral, whose full name is the Catedral Metropolitana de Nuestra Señora de la Asunción. The cathedral stands on the site of the Aztec skull rack (*tzompantli*), where Spanish conqueror Hernán Cortés (see pages 53–4) is said to have found more than 136,000 skulls of sacrificial victims (see page 51). The cathedral took more than 200 years to build and has many architectural styles. Its chief treasure is the elaborate 18th-century Altar of the Kings, with its coloured statues of European kings and queens.

*On the staircase walls of the Palacio Nacional, Mexican artist Diego Rivera painted a series of murals depicting the history of Mexico. In this scene, an important Aztec official sits on a throne before Tenochtitlán and one of its giant causeways.*

To the east of the cathedral is the Templo Mayor, the ruins of the Aztec capital's greatest temple. At its centre is a large stone platform dating from the early 15th century. On the platform is an altar to the Aztec god Huitzilopochtli (see page 52), to whom human sacrifices were made to ensure the Sun rose every day. A modern museum displays statues and artefacts found on the site.

Many of Mexico's major sights are within walking distance of the main square, but some, such as the Museum of Modern Art and Chapultepec Castle, are further away. Buses and taxis ferry tourists around the capital, but by far the best way to travel is by the metro.

West of the Zócalo is **Alameda** Central Park. This was once the place where the Roman Catholic Church burnt heretics in early colonial times. It became a public park in the 16th century and was laid out in the European style with fountains and shady walks. Today, it is a rare and welcome relief from the hustle and bustle of the city's crowded and polluted streets.

Overlooking the park are some of Mexico City's most famous museums and landmarks. The early 20th-century Palacio de Bellas Artes (Palace of Fine Arts) is a large marble building that leans to one side because it is sinking into the marshy ground on which the city is

**The Alameda gets its name from the *álamos* (poplars) with which the park was first planted.**

*Mexico City sprawls haphazardly and uncontrolled across the Valley of Mexico. On the outskirts of the city are heavy industry, dull suburbs and desperately poor shanty towns. There are also former outlying villages and ancient sites, such as the floating gardens at Xochimilco and the Tenayuca and Cuicuilco pyramids. A little further afield are the ruins of Teotihuacán and Tula.*

# AROUND MEXICO CITY

**Because of frequent earthquakes, building highrises in Mexico City is difficult. The Latin American Tower has floating foundations that enable it to survive the tremors.**

built. The museum contains many examples of Mexican mural art, including Rivera's celebrated *Man, Controller of the Universe*. The palace also has a concert hall, which boasts a spectacular stained-glass stage curtain depicting the Mexican landscape. The concert hall is the home of the Ballet Folklórico (see page 99). Close by is the Torre Latino-americana (Latin American Tower). With its 44 storeys, the tower is one of the tallest buildings in the region.

# The floating gardens of Xochimilco

To the south-east of central Mexico City is the village suburb of Xochimilco (*shok-ee-MIL-ko*). In the ancient **Náhuatl** language of the Aztecs, the word '*xochimilco*' meant 'the place where flowers grow'.

Before the Spanish conquest, Indian peoples built rafts of matted mud and reeds (***chiampas***) on the lake here. These were used to grow vegetables, fruit and flowers to sell in the markets of the Aztec capital, Tenochtitlán. Over the centuries, some of these rafts – or floating gardens – became fixed to the bottom of the lake, forming a network of canal-like waterways.

During the conquest, the Spanish set fire to the floating gardens in order to starve the capital of food. The Spanish leader, Hernán Cortés, wrote regretfully that the burning *chiampas* were 'truly a sorrowful sight'. After Cortés's victory, however, the *chiampas* flourished once again, and Xochimilco resumed its old role as the market-garden to the capital.

Today, colourful, decorated gondola-style boats called ***trajineras*** cruise the waterways and can be hired by the hour. Visitors have to be careful, though – some of the boats are very old and may sink! On weekends, ***mariachi*** bands sometimes play on the boats.

A visit to Xochimilco would not be complete without a tour of the beautiful church of San Bernardino. This church dates back to the years following the conquest and has a finely carved relief of St Bernardine with an Indian woman.

*The Independence Monument was erected in 1910 to celebrate the 100th anniversary of the Cry of Dolores (see page 58).*

It takes a whole day to explore the Bosque de Chapultepec – Mexico City's largest park – to the west. Chapultepec, which means 'hill of the grasshoppers', was once the summer residence of the Aztec nobility and lay on the mainland across Lake Texcoco. This beautiful and popular park has a zoo, a theatre and no less than five major museums. Chapultepec Castle – briefly the residence of the Mexican emperor, Maximilian, in the 19th century (see pages 62 and 63) – houses the National Museum of History.

The modern, spacious National Museum of Anthropology has one of the finest collections of Mesoamerican art and objects in the world. The Museum of Modern Art has work by all the major Mexican artists of the 20th century, including muralist Diego Rivera and artist Frida Kahlo (see pages 96–7). The park's zoo is the oldest in the Americas and is said to have been founded by an Aztec emperor.

The Paseo de la Reforma is a wide, busy boulevard that runs north-east to south-west across the city. The famous Independence Monument, a gilded, winged statue of Liberty, known as El Angel, stands on a traffic island on the boulevard. The angel was erected in 1910 at the beginning of the Mexican Revolution. Although it is built on deep, firm foundations, the land around is sinking, so a new step up to the monument has to be added almost every year.

South of the city centre is the University City and the Olympic Stadium, which was built for the 1968 Olympic Games. This vast stadium, decorated with a mosaic by Rivera, is shaped like a volcano and seats 80,000 people. Nearby is the Aztec Stadium – home of Mexican football – which holds 108,500 people.

## Guadalajara: Mexico's most 'Mexican' city

Guadalajara is Mexico's second-largest city and is the capital of the state of Jalisco. Built in a high, fertile valley at 1550 metres (5090 feet), the city enjoys mild, sunny weather all year round and boasts the finest climate in all Central and North America. No wonder its 4 million inhabitants call themselves '*tapatíos*', a name that means 'three times as worthy'. Guadalajara also has the reputation of being Mexico's most Mexican city. Many of the things and traditions that people think of as typically Mexican, such as the drink tequila and the Mexican hat dance (see pages 98–9), were invented here.

Guadalajara is a graceful, modern city, with a grid of broad avenues, sparkling fountains, parks, historic buildings, modern shops and sprawling suburbs. A fleet of trolleybuses ferries people around the city. Many of Guadalajara's important and most interesting sights are clustered in the city centre.

The Spanish founded the city in 1542 and named it after the city in Spain of the same name. At the heart of the old town are four beautiful plazas arranged in a cross shape around the 16th-century cathedral. With its two ornate towers, the cathedral is Guadalajara's most important landmark. On one side of the Plaza de Armas

*Guadalajara is home to some of Mexican painter José Clemente Orozco's most famous works. The murals on the vaulted ceiling of the chapel of the Hospicio Cabañas tell the story of Mexico. On the left, the Spanish king Philip II supports the cross; in the middle, Spaniards on two-headed horses crush some Indians; on the right, a monk converts a native man to Christianity.*

## CENTRAL GUADALAJARA

A Plaza de los Laureles
B Rotonda de los Hombres Ilustres
C Plaza de la Liberación
D Plaza de Armas
E Plazuela de los Mariachis

1 Palace of the Legislature
2 Palace of Justice

City maps in Mexico often mark the site of public buildings called Palacio Municipal and Palacio de Gobierno. These are, respectively, the local and federal government headquarters. The Palacio de Gobierno is sometimes also called the Ayuntamiento.

+ church or cathedral

**The people of Guadalajara like their food. There are hundreds of restaurants in the city, but for a quick meal, people often buy *birria* – tortillas containing beef or lamb in a spicy sauce – from street vendors or in a bar.**

stands the Palacio de Gobierno (Federal Palace). The palace is decorated with frescoes by José Clemente Orozco, one of Mexico's finest muralists (see page 97). The paintings show scenes from Mexico's history, including a portrait of Miguel Hidalgo, the priest who began the campaign for Mexico's independence (see pages 57–8).

Guadalajara's central area includes the 19th-century Teatro Degollado – the town's main theatre – and the Hospicio Cabañas. This former orphanage once housed up to 3000 children, and in 1811, Hidalgo signed a proclamation here against slavery. It is built around 23 courtyards and has a chapel decorated with more of Orozco's powerful murals.

In the large Market Hall nearby, pottery, paper flowers and musical instruments are for sale. Guadalajara is the home of *mariachi* music (see page 98), which is played by strolling musicians. In the Plazuela de los Mariachis, bands of *mariachis* show off their skills. The people of Guadalajara are crazy about football, and the city has no fewer than four professional teams.

## Monterrey: Mexico's American city

The thriving city of Monterrey is the third largest in Mexico, with a population of about 3 million. The capital of the state of Nuevo León, it lies east of the Sierra Madre Oriental in spectacular, craggy mountain scenery. At 540 metres (1770 feet), though, Monterrey's climate can be uncomfortable – hot in summer, cold in winter and dusty all year round.

Monterrey's location near large reserves of iron, oil and coal has made it an important centre of business, and it is the second-largest industrial town in Mexico after the capital. Monterrey produces two-thirds of Mexico's iron and steel and also makes many other goods, including glass, cement, clothing, chemicals and beer. In many ways, the city, with its high-rise city centre, shopping malls and leafy suburbs, is like many large cities in the USA.

Colonists from Spain founded the city at the end of the 16th century and named it after the Spanish viceroy of Mexico, the count of Monterrey. Today, graceful old buildings still stand amid modern sky-scrapers in the town centre.

At the heart of Monterrey is the modern Gran Plaza (Great Square), which locals call the Macro Plaza (Big Square). This vast space, which is more than 1 kilometre (0.6 mile) long, is actually a series of smaller plazas.

The Plaza Cinco de Mayo (5th May), also called the Esplanada de los Héroes (Esplanade of Heroes), has statues of famous figures in Mexico's history. Further south on the Gran Plaza is the impressive Fuente de la Vida (Fountain of Life), which has a statue of a sea god riding a chariot. At the Gran Plaza's southern end is the Plaza Zaragoza, which holds both the cathedral and the

**Monterrey's inhabitants, called *regiomontanos*, are famous for their thrift and business sense.**

## The García Grottos

When the crowds, bustle and heat of Monterrey become too oppressive, its inhabitants like to escape into the wild and beautiful countryside that surrounds the city.

Sometimes they take a trip to the García Grottos – one of the most spectacular cave systems in the Americas. The caves are reached by cable car from the nearby village of Villa García. The caves are floodlit, revealing a brilliant display of stalagmites and stalactites and a freezing-cold underground lake.

39

**The business-oriented city of Monterrey is the cornerstone of the 'Tex-Mex' economy that is developing under NAFTA – the free-trade agreement between Canada, the USA and Mexico.**

extraordinary Beacon of Commerce – a tall, orange concrete slab topped by a powerful laser. Each night, the monument's powerful beam sweeps the city sky.

South of the cathedral is the Río Santa Catarina. The lack of rainfall in Monterrey means that the Santa Catarina's riverbed is usually dry. In 1988, however, after torrential rains, the river burst its banks and flooded the city. More than 200 people drowned.

Monterrey has three large universities, including the Institute of Technology, which is famed throughout Mexico. A bus ride to the west is the Obispado (Bishop's Palace), a fortress on a hill with good views over the town. Today, the palace holds the regional museum.

Monterrey is known for its *norteño*- (northern-) style ranch cooking. The most famous local dish is *cabrito* (whole roasted goat). The city is famous, too, for its excellent beers, which are drunk throughout Mexico. The first brewery – the huge Cerveceria Cuauhtémoc – was founded at the end of the 19th century.

## CENTRAL MONTERREY

During the 1980s, central Monterrey was radically transformed. Forty blocks south of the 5 de Mayo Avenue were demolished in order to join up the two main city squares. The resulting huge plaza, known officially as the Gran Plaza and locally as the Macro Plaza, is Monterrey's modern hub.

**A** Plaza Cinco de Mayo (Esplanada de los Héroes)
**B** Plaza Zaragoza

+ church or cathedral

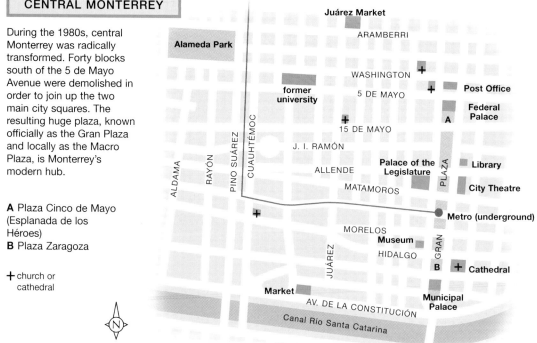

## Puebla: city of angels

Puebla, the fourth-largest city in Mexico, lies south-east of Mexico City. With a population of about 1 million, it is situated in a high valley and has views of the snow-capped peaks of Popocatépetl and Iztaccíhuatl.

Puebla has a strong Spanish flavour and is famous for its old colonial architecture. Some of these old buildings are so richly decorated they look like wedding cakes. The most ornate, called the Almond Cake House, is now the Regional Museum. The city also has more than 70 fine churches, many of which are roofed with bright blue tiles.

Spanish colonists founded Puebla in 1521. At the centre of the old town is the garden-like *zócalo* (main square). The cathedral, the second largest in Mexico, dates back to the 16th century. It has twin towers and a dome with bright tiles. Nearby, the modern Amparo Museum exhibits both Indian and colonial period art, with interactive videos to explain the exhibits.

There are several famous former convents in the centre of Puebla. During the 19th century, the government closed down many church buildings and organizations. The nuns of Santa Mónica ran the convent secretly for nearly 80 years until 1934, when they were betrayed to the authorities. The government suppressed the convent and turned it into a museum of religious art.

In the nearby convent of Santa Rosa, a nun is said to have invented the famous local sauce containing spices and chocolate, called *mole poblano*. Today, the convent

*The city of Puebla is famous for its stunning location. Here the cone-shaped Popocatépetl volcano lets out a harmless plume of smoke on the city skyline.*

## CENTRAL PUEBLA

The names of the streets in Mexico's cities often commemorate the famous heroes and dates from the country's history. The street name '5 de Mayo' recalls the victory over the French at Puebla; '16 de Septiembre' is Independence Day. Historical figures remembered in Puebla include the 20th-century Mexican president Maximino Avila Camacho.

Fort Loreto

State Museum

5 DE MAYO

CALZADA DE LOS FUERTES

Fort Guadalupe

Santa Mónica

Santa Rosa

5 DE MAYO

DEL 5 DE MAYO

HÉROES

Municipal Palace

ZÓCALO

La Compañía

Casa del Alfeñique (Almond Cake House)

Cathedral

University

MAXIMINO AVILA CAMACHO

16 DE SEPTIEMBRE

Amparo Museum

+ church or cathedral

has an excellent museum of popular art.

In the church of La Compañía is the tomb of China Poblana, a 17th-century Asian princess who was captured by pirates and brought to Puebla as a slave. According to legend, her style of dress, with frilly blouse and embroidered skirt, gave rise to the national costume of Mexican women.

North-east of the *zócalo*, crowning a hill, is the modern State Museum, which is largely devoted to archaeology. There are also two old forts – a reminder of the 19th century when the city was often under siege.

Not far from Puebla, on the eastern slopes of Popocatépetl, are the remains of one of the most important cities of ancient Mexico – Cholula. At its height, the city rivalled Teotihuacán (see pages 48 and 50) in size and power. By the time of the conquest, however, the city

**The Spanish first called Puebla Ciudad de los Ángeles (City of Angels).**

**The inhabitants of Puebla are called *poblanos*.**

was under the sway of the Aztecs. During the Spanish conquest, warriors from the city made an unsuccessful attempt to ambush the Spanish leader Hernán Cortés on his way to Tenochtitlán. The Spanish punished the city by demolishing much of it.

The ancient people of Cholula built a huge pyramid, the Pirámide Tepanapa, which was probably dedicated to the god Quetzalcóatl. The pyramid stands almost 60 metres (200 feet) high and is even larger in volume than Egypt's Pyramid of Cheops. Today, though, it is mostly covered with earth, and the domed church of Nuestra Señora de los Remedios crowns its top.

## Puebla's glazed tiles

Puebla is renowned for its brilliant glazed tiles (**azulejos**) that were traditionally used to decorate the roofs, facades and courtyards of the city's churches, convents and houses. The tiles are a good example of how Spanish and Indian traditions have blended together to create something distinctly Mexican. In pre-Hispanic times, the Náhuatl people of the Puebla region were already famous for their colourful glazed pottery. The Aztec emperor Montezuma refused to eat off any other kind! Many of the Spanish colonists who founded Puebla were expert tile-makers. They came from the region around Talavera in central Spain, which was an important tile-making centre. The Indians' sense of colour and design and the colonists' technical know-how combined to make the fine *azulejo* tiles.

# Past and present

*'Also I saw things brought to the king from the New Golden Land [Mexico] … and I marvelled over the subtle ingenuity of the people in these distant lands.'*

German painter Albrecht Dürer, when shown gold objects made by the Aztecs

Mexico's history stretches back many thousands of years. It divides into two parts: before and after 1521, when the Spanish conquered the country. Before then, a series of Native American civilizations flourished in Mexico. The **Olmec, Maya, Aztec** and other native peoples left behind a rich archaeological record of their cultures. Today, ruined cities, vast temple complexes, colourful wall paintings, monumental sculptures and a rich literature bear witness to the wealth and sophistication of these cultures.

After the Spanish conquest, Mexico – then called New Spain – became part of a huge Spanish empire. The native culture was forgotten, destroyed or absorbed, and much of the country was rebuilt in European style. Sometimes, the Spanish colonizers simply built a Spanish city on the ruins of a native one, as at Mexico City. However, in remoter parts of the country, such as the Chiapas Highlands, native cultures survived.

The country only freed itself from Spanish rule in the early 19th century. Since then, Mexico has struggled to carve itself a position in the modern world while in the shadow of its powerful northern neighbour, the USA. Today, Mexico's largely *mestizo* (mixed-race) people have sought to reclaim their pre-Hispanic roots, and many think of themselves as the successors to the great native civilizations.

*A reclining stone figure (chacmool) guards the entrance to a temple at Chichén Itzá. Worshippers used to lay offerings on the figure's stomach.*

## FACT FILE

● The earliest signs of human habitation in Mexico are stone tools found at Tlapacoya, near Mexico City. These date from about 20,000 BC.

● Scholars often divide the ancient civilizations of Mexico into three major periods. The Preclassic period (2500 BC– AD 300) includes the Olmec culture; the Classic (AD 300–900) was characterized by the sophisticated Mayan culture; and the Postclassic (900–1521), by the war-like Aztecs.

● Scholars usually call the civilizations of ancient Mexico and Central America **Mesoamerican** (Central American).

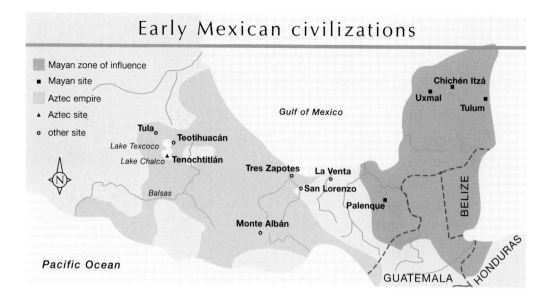

## Early Mexican civilizations

- Mayan zone of influence
- ■ Mayan site
- Aztec empire
- ▲ Aztec site
- ○ other site

Chichén Itzá
Uxmal
Tulum
Gulf of Mexico
Tula
Teotihuacán
Lake Texcoco
Lake Chalco  Tenochtitlán
Tres Zapotes  La Venta
San Lorenzo
Balsas
Palenque
BELIZE
Monte Albán
Pacific Ocean
GUATEMALA  HONDURAS

*Scholars debate whether this huge stone head is a portrait of an Olmec ruler, a warrior or a sportsman.*

## THE EARLY CIVILIZATIONS

The first people to settle in Mexico came originally from Asia. Experts believe that in 40,000 BC or earlier, these people crossed to North America by means of a land bridge that existed across what is now the Bering Strait. From Alaska, they moved gradually south, arriving in Mexico about 20,000 BC. At first, these early groups were wandering hunters. By 3000 BC, however, they had become farmers, growing maize, beans and other crops. Two thousand years later, they were building temples, and their settlements had grown into towns.

### The Olmecs

The Olmecs were the first people to develop an advanced culture in Mexico. Between 1200 and 400 BC, Olmec cities flourished in the forests and swamps of south-east Mexico near the Gulf Coast. The Olmecs devised their own writing and way of counting. Although they had not developed metal tools, they carved giant stone heads to honour their gods, kings and warriors. Important remains of Olmec settlements can be found at La Venta and Tres Zapotes.

## The Maya

The civilization of the Maya, which lasted from 500 BC to AD 1450, was the most advanced of all the native cultures of Mesoamerica. Without metal tools, wheels or pack animals to carry heavy weights, the Maya built beautiful stone cities and temple pyramids decorated with exquisite carvings. Important Mayan sites that can be visited today are Palenque, Uxmal, Chichén Itzá and the ancient trading port of Tulum.

This orderly society was ruled by a priest class. Art and architecture, astronomy and mathematics flourished. The Maya developed a system of writing using pictures, called hieroglyphics, with 500 different symbols carved in stone, and perfected a calendar by which to record important historical events.

At its height, the Mayan empire stretched from the Yucatán Peninsula southwards to Belize, Guatemala and Honduras. From AD 900, however, Mayan culture mysteriously declined. By 1450, the temple cities had been abandoned and were overrun by the rainforest.

### The ball game

Many ancient cities in Mexico had I-shaped ball courts. The ball game played in these courts would have seemed very strange to us today. The game was part entertainment and part religious rite. Teams of players competed to hit a hard, rubber football-sized ball through a stone hoop set high on the wall. Only the players' hips, knees and elbows were allowed to touch the ball. Sometimes, the players played for high stakes: on religious occasions, the losers – or even the winners – were sacrificed to the gods!

*Palenque is one of the most famous of ancient Mayan cities. For a period of about 150 years from the beginning of the 1st century AD, Palenque flourished as a regional capital. The kings and queens of Palenque lived in a magnificent palace.*

# The idea of zero

The Maya were brilliant at maths. Their arithmetic was based on base twenty rather than base ten, which is the system we use today. To write their numbers, they used a system of dots and bars. A dot meant one and a bar meant five. The number eleven was written thus:

To express any number of twenty and above, the Maya used a system of 'places', just as we do. We write the number four hundred and forty-two in figures as 442, where each column represents multiples of 1, 10, 100 and so on. The Maya, however, worked in multiples of 1, 20, 400 and so on, and piled the 'places' on top of each other. Thus the Maya wrote 442 as:

A problem arose with a number such as 401, where there would be a confusing empty space. To solve this, the Maya invented the concept of zero – written:

Four hundred and one was written:

The only other cultures to have invented zero were the Babylonians and the Hindus.

While the Mayan priests were ruling in the east, other cultures were developing in the Oaxaca Valley, in the south-west of Mexico. About 400 BC, the Zapotecs flattened a large mountain top and built the city of Monte Albán. The Zapotecs were great artists and craftspeople, and the Monte Albán site has a series of extraordinary carvings, popularly called the Dancers. Scholars today agree that they depict captured and tortured enemies.

Between about 150 BC and AD 750, a mighty city flourished in the Valley of Mexico. This was Teotihuacán, meaning 'city of the gods'. In the 6th century, this was the largest city in the world and included thousands of homes and a grand ceremonial centre (see page 50).

## The Toltecs

After the fall of Teotihuacán, a warrior people called the Toltecs invaded from the north. The Toltecs dominated the Valley of Mexico from 950 to 1200. Their capital was at Tula, which lies 66 kilometres (41 miles) north of Mexico City.

The Toltecs were skilled builders, weavers and metalworkers. Like other pre-Hispanic peoples, they worshipped many gods and, in particular, Quetzalcóatl. Quetzalcóatl was said to have invented writing and the calendar. He was represented by a snake crowned with the **quetzal** feathers. Toltec influence, including the worship of Quetzalcóatl, spread far and wide. About 1200, however, the Toltecs were conquered by another warrior race – the Aztecs.

# Measuring time

One of the great achievements of the ancient peoples of
Mexico was the invention of a calendar. The Maya seem
to have been the first to develop a system of measuring the
passing of time, in about 400–100 BC. They were farmers
and needed a way to know when to plant their crops. They
also needed to know when to honour the friendly gods and
when to appease the unfriendly ones. The Mayan calendar was
adopted by other Mesoamerican people, including the Aztecs.

The cogwheels show how the Mayan calendar worked.
There were two main systems for counting days, which were
used together to make the so-called **Calendar Round**. The first
system – the Sacred Year – was based on a 260-day 'year', in
which each day had both a number from one to thirteen
attached to it as well as one of twenty different name days.
Each day had its own special god, and children were named
according to which cycle and name day they were born on.

There was also a solar, 365-day calendar like our own. This
year was divided into eighteen 'months' of twenty days
each, plus five 'unhappy' (Uayeb) days. Each month
began with a 'Seating' day. The 365-day and
260-day years ran at
the same time to
produce a 52-
solar-year
cycle,
called the
Calendar
Round.
Ancient
peoples
feared the
completion of
this cycle, and
celebrated it with
special rites to ward off the end of the world.

**SACRED MONTHS**
1. Earth Monster
2. Wind
3. Darkness
4. Ripe Maize
5. Serpent
6. Death
7. Hand
8. Venus
9. Water
10. Dog
11. Monkey
12. Bad Rain
13. Growing Maize
14. Jaguar
15. Moon
16. Wax
17. Earth
18. Blade
19. Rain
20. Lord

**SACRED YEAR**

**SOLAR YEAR**

The Calendar Round date

SEATING OF POP

**SOLAR MONTHS**

POP
UO
ZIP
ZOTZ
TZEC
ZUL
YAXKIN
MOL
CHEN
YAX
ZAC
CEH
MAC
KANKIN
MUAN
PAX
KAYAB
CUMKU

14 POP, 13 POP, 12 POP, 11 POP, 10 POP, 9 POP, 8 POP, 7 POP, 6 POP, 5 POP, 4 POP, 3 POP, 2 POP, 1 POP, 4 UAYEB, 3 UAYEB, 2 UAYEB, 1 UAYEB, SEATING OF UAYEB, 19 CUMKU, 18 CUMKU, CUMKU, KU

# Who built Teotihuacán?

No one is quite sure who built and lived in the great city of Teotihuacán, the ruins of which lie in the Valley of Mexico, 50 km (30 miles) north-east of Mexico City. For centuries, it was the largest and most important city in the pre-Hispanic Americas, exerting an influence for hundreds of kilometres around. The city rose to prominence in about AD 150, and at its height had a population of a quarter of a million people. Its religious and administrative centre was based on a great road – the so-called Way of the Dead – running roughly north–south for 2.4 km (1.5 miles).

At the northern end of the Way of the Dead was the Pyramid of the Moon, and at the southern, the temple of the god Quetzalcóatl. Along the way was the huge Pyramid of the Sun. This measures 220 by 232 m (720 by 760 ft) at its base and rises in five massive tiers to a height of 66 m (216 ft). Here the Pyramid of the Sun and the Way of the Dead are seen from the Pyramid of the Moon.

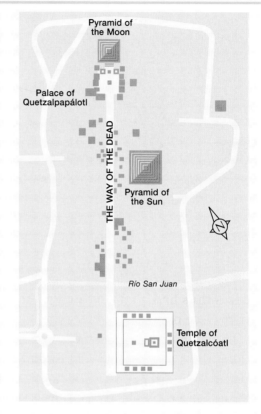

Invaders sacked Teotihuacán in about AD 650 – a disaster from which it never recovered. Today, the city is the most visited ancient site in the Americas.

## The Aztecs

The Aztecs were the last of the great ancient cultures. They arrived from the north-west in about 1300 and built their capital, Tenochtitlán, on an island in the Texcoco Lake in the Valley of Mexico. The Aztecs conquered all the neighbouring peoples and made them pay a yearly tribute of gold or silver treasure. By 1500, they controlled an empire of 38 provinces and some 5 million people, stretching from the Pacific Ocean to the Gulf of Mexico.

Despite their war-like temperament, the Aztecs also led a cultivated and orderly city life. Their staple food was maize, which grew abundantly and needed little labour. The Aztecs thus had a lot of time for art, poetry (see page 97) and religion.

The harmony of Aztec society makes their practice of human sacrifice all the more shocking. The Aztecs worshipped many gods, but principally they worshipped a fierce sun god called Huitzilopochtli, to whom they sacrificed thousands of people every year (see page 32).

## The Aztec gods

The peoples of Mesoamerica were deeply religious. They depicted their gods in their paintings, sculptures, pottery and architecture, and lived in dread of the gods' anger. Daily life was marked by many religious ceremonies.

The Aztecs were no exception. They worshipped about 126 major gods, and nearly every act, craft, day, month and city had its own special god. Very often, gods were worshipped in pairs – one male and one female.

The Aztecs associated the gods with different colours and compass points. The god Quetzalcóatl, for example, was associated with the colour white and the west.

## SPANISH CONQUEST AND RULE

In 1492, the Genoese explorer Christopher Columbus (1451–1506) became the first European to record his arrival in the Americas. He claimed the lands he found in the name of Spain, whose king he served. The Spanish called the 'new world' the Indies (*las Indias*) and its inhabitants Indians because Columbus believed he had landed in Asia, then loosely called India.

By 1517, Spanish explorers arrived in what is now Mexico and learnt of the Aztec empire to the west, with its wealth of gold, silver and jewels.

# Human sacrifice

When the Spanish first encountered the Aztecs in 1519, they were horrified to discover that this otherwise civilized people practised human sacrifice.

The Aztecs, however, believed that the shedding of human blood was necessary to keep the Sun alive. As each dawn approached, priests held a victim down on a stone block and cut out his still-beating heart. One priest would then show the heart to the Sun, while successful warriors ate the victim's limbs.

In the decades before the Spanish arrival, the numbers of people sacrificed increased dramatically, and the Aztec emperors waged war almost continuously to capture enough victims for their sacrifices. This war was known as the Flowery War. On one occasion, during the dedication of the main temple of Tenochtitlán in 1487, 20,000 captives were sacrificed.

The Maya and Aztecs produced many painted 'books', which scholars call codices (the singular is 'codex'). Before the Spanish conquest, codices were made out of cotton or skins, folded into pleats or in a roll. After the conquest, codices were painted on paper and usually included Spanish rather than Aztec text. This 16th-century Spanish-Aztec codex shows a human sacrifice.

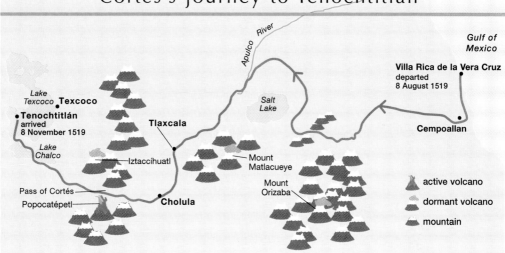

## Cortés's journey to Tenochtitlán

## The conquest

In 1519, a Spanish adventurer named Hernán Cortés (1485–1547) set off for the Aztec capital, Tenochtitlán, spurred on by stories of gold. Cortés had horses and a small army of 300 conquistadors (soldiers) armed with guns and cannon. He was soon joined by many native warriors from peoples who had been conquered by the Aztecs and who hated their Aztec lords.

When they reached Tenochtitlán, the Spanish were amazed by the beauty of the Aztec city on the lake. They marvelled at its temples, floating gardens (see page 35) and the causeways that linked the island to the mainland. In turn, the Aztecs were awed by the Spanish. They had never seen white people, horses or guns before.

The Aztec emperor, Montezuma (1466–1520), believed that Cortés, with his prancing horse and glittering armour, was Quetzalcóatl who had returned to rule the Aztecs. Instead of fighting the Spanish, he welcomed them and presented them with gifts. Cortés, however, betrayed the emperor's trust and placed him under arrest.

In 1520, Cortés was called away to the coast. In his bsence, the conquistadors grew nervous and, during a religious ceremony, attacked and murdered some 200

*The red line shows Cortés's journey from Villa Rica de la Vera Cruz to Tenochtitlán – a distance as the crow flies of some 435 kilometres (270 miles). The difficult journey through rainforest, desert and mountains, and through sometimes hostile cities, took three months to complete.*

*This mural by Roberto Cuevo del Río depicts the meeting of Cortés and Montezuma.*

Aztec noblemen. The Aztec people rose up against the Spanish invaders, and in the confusion, Montezuma was killed. The Spanish and their Indian allies fled the city, although not before hundreds had been slaughtered. The event is remembered as the *Noche Triste* – the Sad Night.

The following year, Cortés returned with some 900 Spanish soldiers and a large army of Indian warriors. He also brought ships, which were carried across land in sections and then reassembled on the shores of Lake Texcoco. The Spanish-led army was able to surround Tenochtitlán from both land and water and cut off its supplies of food. At first, the Aztecs, now led by the emperor Cuauhtémoc (1495–1525), were able to beat back the Spanish assault. In August 1521, however, after a siege of 75 days, Cuauhtémoc – the last Aztec emperor – surrendered to the Spanish. The once great Aztec empire became a Spanish colony, and the beautiful city of Tenochtitlán was razed.

## Conversion and cruelty

For the next 300 years, Mexico was officially part of the Spanish empire. The Spanish king's representative, the viceroy, was the highest authority in the land. The Indians were allowed to speak their own languages and to keep some of their own laws and customs, but they had to pay a 'tribute' – *encomienda* – in the form of work. Gradually, hundreds of Spanish missionaries arrived to convert the

Indians to the Roman Catholic religion. The missionaries were largely Franciscans, whose gentleness and humility won the respect of the Indian peoples and helped bring about their swift and bloodless conversion. A Dominican priest, Bartolomé de Las Casas, became a passionate defender of Indian rights (see page 56).

The civilian authorities in the new colony were not so kind. The Spanish conquerors razed the Indian cities and plundered the country's rich supply of gold and silver. Indians and imported African slaves worked on the land and down the mines in terrible conditions. On large estates called **haciendas**, Spanish landowners usually treated the Indians badly. Tens of thousands of Indians died of diseases, such as smallpox, that had previously been unknown in the New World.

During the 16th century, the Spanish conquistadors led expeditions north in search of riches. They occupied land in what are now the US states of Texas, California, Arizona and New Mexico. New Spain became the second-largest country in the Americas after Brazil.

**By 1800, the Spanish had built more than 12,000 churches in Mexico.**

## New Spain in 1784

CANADA

San Francisco
•
CALIFORNIA

VICEROYALTY
OF NEW SPAIN

UNITED
STATES
OF
AMERICA

New Orleans
•

ATLANTIC OCEAN

FLORIDA

Havana
•

Guadalajara •
⊛ •Veracruz
Mexico City
Acapulco •
Guatemala •

CUBA

SANTO
DOMINGO

PACIFIC OCEAN

VICEROYALTY OF
NEW GRANADA

*In the 18th century, the Spanish empire in the Americas was vast, stretching from the present-day US–Canadian border to the tip of South America. The northern part – of which Mexico City was the hub – formed the Viceroyalty of New Spain (Nueva España).*

55

# 'The apostle of the Indians'

The Spanish conquerors inflicted great cruelties on the conquered peoples of Mexico. Their cruelty did not go uncriticized, however. One figure, in particular, stands out in protesting against the maltreatment of the Indian peoples and the wanton destruction of their culture: the priest Bartolomé de Las Casas (1474–1566), nicknamed 'the apostle of the Indians'.

Las Casas first came to America as a soldier and took part in the invasion of Cuba. He also preached to convert the Indians to Roman Catholicism. As a reward for his services, the Spanish gave him land and Indian serfs.

In 1514, La Casas gave a famous sermon in which he attacked the Spanish oppression of the Indians. The following year, he returned to Spain to plead the Indians' cause with the king, Charles I. He persuaded the king to set up settlements in what is now Venezuela in which Indians and Spaniards would live together on equal terms. The plan failed when Spanish landowners in America objected. Las Casas; however, fought on.

In his *Very Brief Account of the Destruction of the Indies*, published after his death, Las Casas angrily exposed the murder, rape and forced conversion that the Spanish inflicted on the Indians. He argued, too, for the restitution (return) of land to the native peoples. Editions of Bartolomé de Las Casas's text were often illustrated with gruesome depictions of the tortures inflicted on the Indians.

Las Casas was an inspirational figure for liberation theology, the 20th-century movement of Roman Catholic clergy that continues to fight for human rights throughout Latin America.

## INDEPENDENCE

By 1800, Indian peoples made up about 30 per cent of Mexico's population. They were mostly very poor and had few rights. Next up the social scale were the *mestizos*, mixed-race descendants of Spanish and Indian ancestors. Both Indians and *mestizos* sometimes worked as bonded labourers (*peones*), who were tied by debt to their employers.

The *criollos* (creoles) were whites born of Spanish parents in the colony. They formed a middle class and often owned large estates or mines. They resented having to pay taxes to the Spanish Crown and wanted political power to match their economic power. A tiny minority of Spanish-born whites owned the vast majority of Mexico's land and held all the power. They were called *peninsulares*, meaning 'people from the [Iberian] peninsula'. In 1800, there were just 40,000 of them in a population of 6 million whites and 3 million Indians. Only *peninsulares* could hold office.

The king of Spain, meanwhile, was too busy with his country's own troubles to do much about the injustice and corruption that were leading his colony into crisis.

### Hidalgo and the Grito de Dolores

The American Declaration of Independence (1776) and the French Revolution (1789) inspired *criollo* Mexicans to fight for independence for their country. The first open call for independence came from a *criollo* priest named Miguel Hidalgo y Costilla (1753–1811).

On 16 September 1810, Hidalgo made a rousing speech from the balcony of his church in Dolores in central Mexico. In his speech, he called upon all Mexicans to rebel against Spanish rule. Hidalgo gathered support, and he was

**Experts estimate that the native population in central Mexico fell by some 90 per cent after the Spanish conquest.**

## Independence Day

Each year, at midnight on the eve of Mexico's Independence Day – 16 September – the Mexican president and politicians all over the country shout the Grito de Dolores – '¡Mexicanos, Viva México!' – 'Mexicans! Long live Mexico!' This was the cry with which Hidalgo completed his angry speech on the balcony of his church at Dolores.

As soon as the president has issued this cry, the Independence Day celebrations can begin.

*José Clemente Orozco's mural for the Palacio de Gobierno in Guadalajara shows Miguel Hidalgo angrily brandishing the torch of independence.*

able to occupy the important city of Guadalajara and to set up a provisional government.

Unfortunately, Hidalgo was unable to control the rebellion that he had helped unleash. His undisciplined *mestizo* and Indian soldiers carried out a series of bloody massacres of the *peninsulares*, and the Mexican *criollos*, who had at first supported the uprising, now turned against it. In 1811, Spanish troops captured and soon after executed the hapless Hidalgo.

Hidalgo is today honoured as a great Mexican hero, and almost every city and town has a road or square named after him. The town of Dolores is now called Dolores Hidalgo in his memory, and its church bells are rung just once a year – on Independence Day.

## The revolt continues

In 1813, another revolt was led by another priest, José María Morelos y Pavón (1765–1815). By 1813, he controlled almost all of the country except for Mexico City. At the Congress of Chilpancingo, he declared Mexico's independence from Spain and issued a constitution that abolished slavery and introduced equality of the races. Government forces rapidly defeated the rebels, however. Morelos was quickly executed, and the Spanish king increased taxes and raised a large army to put down any further trouble.

In 1821, the Spanish sent an army commanded by a *mestizo* officer named Agustín de Iturbide (1783–1824) to crush the rebel forces, which were now led by Vicente Guerrero (1783–1824). By this time, the Mexican *criollos* had turned against the Spanish, too. In Spain itself, there were liberal reforms that threatened the privileges of the ruling classes, and the *criollos* worried that similar reforms would take place in Mexico.

Finding the odds stacked so overwhelmingly against the Spanish, Iturbide made peace with Guerrero, and the two armies joined forces. The movement for Mexican independence was now unstoppable. In 1821, the Treaty of Córdoba gave Mexico its independence.

The early years of independence were a time of turmoil in Mexico. Little changed for ordinary people, and it seemed as if Mexico had simply exchanged one set of rulers for another. At first, Iturbide ruled Mexico as emperor but was quickly deposed. Mexico was declared a republic, and an old revolutionary, Guadalupe Victoria (1786–1843), became the first president.

From 1833 to 1855, an ambitious and vain general named Antonio López de Santa-Anna was the dominant force in Mexican politics, first as president, then as dictator of Mexico. Santa-Anna was to have an influential role in shaping modern Mexico.

Iturbide was crowned emperor in a ceremony in Mexico City cathedral in 1822. The crown was too small for Iturbide's head, and the president of Mexico's new parliament whispered to the emperor, 'Your Majesty must not let the crown fall.' Iturbide whispered back, 'It shall not!'

## The mummified leg of Santa-Anna

President Santa-Anna is one of Mexico's larger-than-life historical figures. He was undoubtedly a courageous soldier. His defeat of a small Spanish invasion force at Tampico in 1829 made him a national hero and enabled him to have himself elected Mexican president in 1833. His success seems to have gone to his head, however.

In 1839, Santa-Anna lost a leg while fighting the French. The leg was carefully mummified and buried. In 1842, he had the leg dug up and paraded through the streets of Mexico City, much as if it were a holy relic. Today, Santa-Anna is chiefly remembered as the man who presided over the loss of more than half of Mexico's territory.

Some Texan cities recall the heroes of the state's struggle for independence from Mexico. Houston, for, example, is named after Sam Houston, who led the Texan attack at San Jacinto.

*Santa-Anna directs the Mexican troops against the Spanish at Tampico. Santa Anna's triumph made him a hero for the Mexican people.*

## Mexico's shrinking territory

In the 1800s, Mexican territory stretched far north of the Río Bravo into Texas and California. The Mexican government encouraged settlers from North America to go and live there because so few people lived on the land. By 1830, however, the people of Texas began to seek freedom from Mexico.

In 1836, Texas broke away and proclaimed its independence. Santa-Anna led 7000 men north to crush the revolt. At the Battle of the Alamo in March 1836 in San Antonio, he defeated Texan forces and killed the men defending the settlers' fort of El Alamo.

Santa-Anna did not enjoy his victory for long. A month later, Texan forces routed the Mexican army at the San Jacinto River. Santa-Anna was forced to recognize the independence of Texas, which at that time included parts of Colorado, New Mexico and even Wyoming. In 1846, Texas became part of the USA.

Skirmishes between the USA and Mexico continued, however. Finally, these disputes led to a war that lasted for two years. In 1846, US forces occupied Mexican territory north of the Río Bravo. The following year, an

army led by General Winfield Scott stormed and occupied Mexico City. In 1848, Mexico was forced to sign the humiliating Treaty of Guadalupe Hidalgo. Under this treaty, the USA was granted most of what are now the states of California, Nevada, Arizona, New Mexico, Utah and Wyoming at a cost of about 9 million pounds.

In 1853, the USA went on to make the so-called Gadsden Purchase, buying more land in Arizona and New Mexico from Mexico for about 6 million pounds. In all, in the years following independence, Mexico lost half its territory to the USA.

## Mexico's changing borders

- San Francisco

PACIFIC
OCEAN

Gulf of Mexico

- – 1824 border
- territory lost in 1846    Mexico City
- territory lost in 1848
- territory lost in 1853
- Mexico's territory today

*Between 1824 and 1853, Mexico lost more than half of its territory to the USA.*

## Civil war and the French invasion

After Santa-Anna's defeat, the liberals gained support in Mexico. Power and most of the country's wealth and land still lay in the hands of a few white people and the Roman Catholic Church. Many Indians and *mestizos* lived in poverty. In 1858, a liberal lawyer named Benito Juárez (1806–72) was elected president. Juárez was a Zapotec Indian from Oaxaca. He was a just man with high ideals, and he is sometimes compared to US President Abraham Lincoln.

After his election, Juárez began an ambitious programme of reform. His aims were to curb the power of the church and army and to help the poor. Juárez's government confiscated and sold the vast lands owned by the church and took away church and army privileges.

The conservatives, however, rebelled against these sweeping changes. A civil war, called the War of the Reform, broke out. The conservatives took Mexico City, and Juárez was forced to flee and set up government in Veracruz, on the east coast. By 1861, however, the

**Juárez is Mexico's greatest national hero. The city of El Paso del Norte on the Río Bravo was named Ciudad Juárez (City of Juárez) in his honour.**

## Maximilian's execution

The fall of the hapless emperor Maximilian (1832–67) moved many famous Europeans to appeal to President Juárez to spare his life. Many French people felt particularly responsible for his fate because it was the French emperor Napoleon III who had schemed to have Maximilian placed on the Mexican throne and then abandoned him to his fate.

Despite the pleas for mercy, Juárez had Maximilian executed by firing squad on a hill outside the city of Querétaro. The emperor was fiercely loyal to his adopted country, and he died declaring, 'May my blood flow for the good of this land. Viva [long live] Mexico.'

The French artist Edouard Manet (1832–83) was deeply moved by the emperor's fate and painted the scene of his execution four times. This painting is the first version of 1867 and today hangs in the Boston Museum of Fine Arts in the USA. It shows all the drama and horror of the execution. In later versions, Manet showed the firing squad wearing French, not Mexican, uniforms. In this way, he showed Napoleon's responsibility for Maximilian's death.

liberals had once again triumphed over the conservatives, and Juárez was able to return to the capital.

The civil war left the Mexican economy in ruins. The country owed large sums to Spain, France and Britain. Juárez decided to delay repayment on these debts for two years to let the economy recover.

In 1862, the three European nations sent armies to Mexico to collect their debts. While the British and Spanish forces soon withdrew, the French emperor, Napoleon III, launched an invasion. At first, the Mexicans were able to resist the French, and on 5 May, General Ignacio Zaragoza won a spectacular victory over the mighty French army at Puebla.

The triumph at Puebla was only a temporary check to the French advance. Later that same year, Napoleon occupied Mexico City and installed an Austrian archduke, Maximilian, as emperor. Maximilian's rule lasted just three years. In 1866, pressure from the USA and war in Europe forced the French to withdraw. Juárez returned to the capital, and the emperor Maximilian was executed (see box opposite).

**Mexico still celebrates 5th May as a national holiday – Cinco de Mayo.**

## Ruled by a dictator

After the death of Juárez in 1872, a *mestizo* general named Porfirio Díaz (1830–1915) became president in 1876. Díaz remained in power for most of the next 35 years until 1911. At first, Díaz supported the ideals of Juárez, but eventually he became a ruthless dictator who silenced opposition by force.

The period of Díaz's dictatorship, called the Porfiriato, was a time of peace for Mexico. With the help of foreign investment, the country was modernized. Railways and new roads were built and telephone lines installed. Mining and the oil industry prospered, too.

Only a few wealthy Mexicans and foreign business people profited from the peace, and Mexico's land and wealth were still owned by a tiny handful of people. Indians and poor *mestizos* now owned even less land.

**During the Porfiriato, Mexico's railway system expanded from 639 km (397 miles) of track in 1876 to 23,950 km (14,880 miles) in 1910.**

**In 1910, 3 to 4 per cent of the population owned all of Mexico's land.**

*The simple but passionate ideals of the revolutionary hero Emiliano Zapata are still influential in Mexico today.*

## REVOLUTION IN MEXICO

During the early 1900s, opposition to Porfirio Díaz grew. In 1910, a liberal landowner called Francisco Madero (1873–1913) ran for president. He would have won had not Díaz jailed him during the election campaign. After his release, Madero called for a revolution to overthrow the dictator.

On 20 November, revolutionary groups all over Mexico took up arms and fought the government. In the north, they were led by the fearsome Francisco 'Pancho' Villa (1877–1923), who had been a Robin Hood-style bandit chief. In the south, the handsome and idealistic guerrilla leader Emiliano Zapata (1879–1919) called for the land to be divided among the peasants and rallied revolutionaries everywhere with the rousing cry '*Tierra y Libertad*' – 'Land and Freedom'.

In 1911, Díaz was forced to resign to stop the bloodshed, and Madero was elected president. Madero was immediately faced with the difficult task of reconciling the moderate and radical factions of the revolution. Moderates like himself wanted only to stop the worst abuses of the old regime; radicals, like Zapata, wanted to divide the great hacienda estates among the peasants. Right-wing counter-revolutionaries, who feared the loss of their lands, also plotted against the new republic.

In 1913, fighting broke out between the counter-revolutionaries and the government. The unrest lasted for ten days, during which time thousands of civilians were killed. The USA intervened on the side of the rebels, Madero was deposed and executed, and his former general, Victoriano Huerta (1854–1916), seized power and became president.

# MEXICO DURING THE REVOLUTION

The bandit Francisco Villa leads revolts in the northern states of Chihuahua and Sonora.

Columbus

Venustiano Carranza, governor of the state of Coahuila, leads moderate opposition to the counter-revolutionary regime.

Atlantic Ocean

The USA invades Veracruz in support of Carranza in 1914.

Querétaro

A convention at the city of Querétaro in 1916–17 forms Mexico's new revolutionary constitution.

Pacific Ocean

MEXICO CITY

Veracruz

Emiliano Zapata takes up arms in support of the poor in the state of Morelos.

N

Once again, the rebels united against a reactionary regime. Madero's followers, including the moderates Venustiano Carranza (1859–1920) and General Álvaro Obregón (1880–1928), united with Villa and Zapata against Huerta. Carranza took Mexico City in 1914, and Huerta fled. At this point, the old divisions between moderates and radicals re-emerged and the country fell into a bitter civil war that lasted for the next six years.

With the support of the USA, Carranza became president and in 1917 produced a new constitution for Mexico (see page 67). The government was committed to redistributing land to the peasants. The constitution created at Querétaro set out basic rights for workers and recognized trades unions. It aimed to reform education, control farms and the oil industry and reduce the power of the Catholic Church. It also limited the rule of presidents to just one term of office – six years.

Carranza stifled his radical opposition by having Zapata assassinated in 1919, but in the following year, was himself assassinated in an otherwise bloodless revolt led by his former comrade General Obregón. Altogether more than a million people died during the ten years of revolution.

*The map above shows the main areas of opposition to the government during the revolution.*

*The US 'Wanted' poster below dates from 1916, when Villa raided Columbus, New Mexico, in the hope of bringing the USA and Carranza's regime into conflict.*

PROCLAMATION $5,000.00 REWARD

FRANCISCO (PANCHO) VILLA

ALSO $1,000. REWARD FOR ARREST OF CANDELARIO CERVANTES, PABLO LOPEZ, FRANCISCO BELTRAN, MARTIN LOPEZ

ANY INFORMATION LEADING TO HIS APPREHENSION WILL BE REWARDED.

CHIEF OF POLICE
Columbus
New Mexico

MARCH 9, 1916

*After the revolution, art had a role to play in educating the Mexican people and shaping the values of the new society. This detail of a mural by David Siqueiros shows peasant followers of Villa and Zapata.*

## Reform after revolution

Obregón now became president and began to institute the reform programme set out in the 1917 constitution. He gave land to the peasants and built more than a thousand schools. The new government also encouraged the arts, commissioning such artists as Diego Rivera and David Siqueiros to paint murals for new public buildings.

The reforms continued under President Plutarco Elías Calles (1877–1945), who was elected in 1924. Calles also took measures against the Roman Catholic Church, closing down monasteries and church schools. In 1929, Calles formed the National Revolutionary Party (Partido de la Revolución Mexicana, or PRM). The party remained in power until 2000, although it changed its name to the Institutional Revolutionary Party (Partido Revolucionario Institucional, or PRI) in 1946.

In 1934, Lázaro Cárdenas (1895–1970) became president. For the first time, the government was not headed by a leader who had fought in the revolution. Cárdenas was an energetic president who continued with the reforms of his predecessors. He strengthened the trade unions and distributed much more land to the peasants. In 1938, following a strike by workers in the oil industry, his government seized control of British and US oil companies in Mexico and formed the mighty Mexican Petroleum Company, or PEMEX (see page 81). This act laid down the basis for the modern Mexican economy.

With the election of Manuel Avila Camacho in 1940, Mexico entered a much more conservative period of government after two decades of frenetic reform.

## AFTER WORLD WAR TWO

Mexican industry grew by leaps and bounds during World War Two (1939–45). In 1942, Mexico entered the war on the side of the Allies – Britain, France and the USA – and sent workers and materials across the northern border to help win the war. Mexican factories also produced war equipment, and the economy boomed. After the war finished, industry and agriculture continued to expand during the 1950s and 1960s, and roads and railways improved.

The year 1968 was a time of unrest for students and young people in many countries. That year, Mexico was host to the Olympic Games. In Mexico City, students demonstrated on the streets to protest against the large amounts of money being spent on the games. The army acted to put down the demonstration. Troops opened fire and some 400 students were killed.

During the 1970s, Mexico struggled to maintain progress at a time of worldwide economic recession (slowdown). When vast reserves of oil were discovered in the

## The 1917 constitution

According to Carranza's constitution of 1917, the government had a duty to intervene actively to promote the social, economic and cultural welfare of all Mexico's citizens. Besides affirming civil liberties, such as the freedom of speech, the constitution included the following important articles:

**Article 3** secular, free, compulsory state education
**Article 14** the right to private property
**Article 27** national ownership of mineral resources, such as silver and oil; minimum wages and the right to strike; the fair distribution of land
**Article 123** a national social security system, including health and welfare programmes.

**On 19 September 1985, two big earthquakes shook southern Mexico and Mexico City. More than 8000 people died, and 100,000 were made homeless.**

country, Mexico borrowed large sums of money from foreign investors to help develop the oil industry. In the 1980s, the price of oil fell worldwide, which led to a financial crisis in Mexico. The situation worsened when thousands of refugees arrived in Chiapas, fleeing wars in Central America – in Nicaragua and El Salvador.

In 1988, political parties opposing the PRI gained popular support during the election campaign of that year. Carlos Salinas de Gortari of the PRI won the election but only just. Aiming to ease Mexico's financial problems, President Salinas encouraged foreign investment and cut public spending.

### The end of PRI rule

Mexico's major trading partner was and continues to be the USA – three-quarters of Mexico's **imports** and **exports** are traded with its powerful neighbour. In 1993, President Salinas negotiated an important trade treaty,

## Mexican migration to the USA

The earliest Mexican Americans, (*chicanos*) did not move to the USA but were conquered. Under the Treaty of Guadelupe Hidalgo of 1848, Mexico gave up a huge block of land to the USA. The US government gave Mexican citizens living in the area the right to become US citizens or leave for Mexico.

Since then, millions of Mexicans have migrated to the USA in search of work and better pay. The USA depends on Mexico as a source of cheap labour. In the 1890s, for example, the American West and California recruited Mexicans to work on farms, railway building and food factories. Despite the low wages

paid to Mexican immigrants, the wages were higher than those paid in Mexico. The downside was that in times of economic slowdown, Mexican workers were deported.

Today, there are huge Mexican communities in the USA, particularly in California. Between 1981 and 1995, 3 million Mexicans moved – often illegally – to the USA – the equivalent of 20% of Mexico's population growth. Today, there are thought to be more than 3 million illegal Mexican immigrants in the USA. For years, the immigrant problem has caused difficult relations between the two countries (see pages 21 and 116).

the North American Free Trade Agreement (NAFTA), with the USA and Canada. The agreement created a vast free-trade zone in which goods could be traded without duties. The agreement gave a boost to the Mexican economy that should last well into the 21st century.

President Salinas's trade policy was successful, but there were troubles at home. In 1994, the Zapatista National Liberation Army, which was made up of

The Chiapas rebellion

towns seized in Chiapas by the Zapatistas in January 1994

Indian revolutionaries from the Chiapas Highlands, revolted against the government (see page 70) and occupied cities and land. Many of Mexico's poor were worried that NAFTA would make them still poorer.

In 1994, Ernesto Zedillo Ponce de León of the PRI was elected president by the narrowest margin in Mexican history – winning only 49 per cent of the vote. There was widespread dissatisfaction with the party's rule. In September 1994, the PRI secretary general, José Francisco Ruiz Massieu, was murdered. In 1997, the PRI lost control of both the Chamber of Deputies (the parliament's lower house) and the mayorality of Mexico City. In 2000, the PRI lost the presidency when Vincente Fox Quesada of the National Action Party was elected.

*In 1994, Chiapas – Mexico's poorest state – experienced a wave of violent unrest that plunged the whole country into deep crisis.*

## THE GOVERNMENT OF MEXICO

Mexico is a federal republic with a democratic form of government. The country is divided into 31 states and one federal district, which contains the capital, Mexico City. Each state is administered by an elected governor and is divided into townships.

# The 1994 Zapatista rebellion

On the same day that the NAFTA agreement came into effect, a group of mask-clad guerrillas from the Zapatista National Liberation Army seized control of several towns in the poor and Indian-dominated state of Chiapas, in southern Mexico. The Zapatistas named themselves after the most radical leader of the Mexican Revolution, Emiliano Zapata. They were protesting against their poverty and lack of rights. 'We possess nothing,' their manifesto declared, 'absolutely nothing, no home, no land, no work, no education.'

The government responded heavy-handedly, sending in troops and aircraft against only lightly armed men. There was an international outcry at the government's brutality, and on 8 January, the Mexican president, Carlos Salinas, was forced to offer the Zapatistas a truce and a negotiated settlement. The peace talks soon broke down, however. By the beginning of the 21st century, the crisis remained unresolved. The Zapatistas continued to occupy land in Chiapas and to have the support of local people.

Mexico's constitution is quite similar to that of the USA. The parliament, called the National Congress, is where the government decides policies, makes laws and controls taxes. Congress has two houses, the Senate and the Federal Chamber of Deputies. The Senate has 128 members who are elected for six years and half of whom are replaced every three years. The Chamber of Deputies has 500 members, elected every three years.

Mexico's president is head of state and of the government. He appoints a Council of Ministers (Cabinet) and senior state officials, such as the governor of Mexico

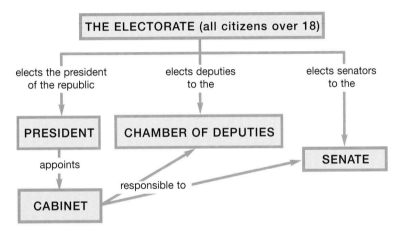

*Mexico is a multi-party democracy. However, until recently, the predominance of a single party – the PRI – meant that in practice the president wielded almost total power over government.*

City, and introduces many laws. The president of Mexico has great power, but can serve only one term of office, which lasts six years (see pages 68 and 69).

Until recently, the Institutional Revolutionary Party (PRI) was the most important party in Mexico. It was founded in 1929 and for a long time it held an iron grip on political power. This meant that while Mexico was in theory a multi-party democracy, in practice it was a one-party state. What is more, the outgoing PRI president usually chose his successor – a practice called *dedazo* ('touching with the finger').

In 2000, however, the PRI's 71-year hold on power was ended when the leader of the conservative National Action Party (PAN), Vincente Fox Quesada, was elected president. Many Mexicans welcomed the fact that the

**All Mexicans aged eighteen and over can vote in elections. Voting is compulsory but not enforced (people are not fined). Women gained the vote in all elections only in 1953.**

## THE MEXICAN PARLIAMENT IN 2002

**President** Vincente Fox Quesada

**Federal Chamber of Deputies**
500 members • last election 2000 • elections held every 3 years

AC (Alliance for Change) 38%
PRI (Institutional Revolutionary Party) 37%
AM (Alliance for Mexico) 19%
others 6%

**Senate**
128 members • last election 2000 • senators elected for 6 years

AC (Alliance for Change) 38%
PRI (Institutional Revolutionary Party) 37%
AM (Alliance for Mexico) 20%
others 7%

political dominance of the PRI was finally at an end.
When President Fox swept to power, he promised that
the one-party rule was over, and also pledged to wipe
out the widespread corruption that had been evident
during the PRI regime. Today, after years of right-wing
rule, many Mexicans are impatient to see these changes
take effect.

## PEOPLE AND SOCIETY

For almost 500 years, Mexico has been a melting pot
where many races have met and mingled. Today, most
of the population – about 60 per cent – are *mestizos*, the
mixed-race descendants of Spanish and Indian ancestors. Being *mestizo* is a subject of national pride.

Indian groups now make up only about 30 per cent of
the population (see box opposite). Most Indians live
either in Chiapas and Oaxaca, in southern Mexico, or in
the Yucatán, in the east. There are more than 50 different
Indian groups. These range from major ethnic groups,
such as the Nahua and the Maya, to lesser groups, such as
the Huichol. There are also whites, mainly *criollos* –
whites born in Mexico (about 9 per cent). Africans and
Asians make up 1 per cent of the population.

# Mexico's Indian peoples today

After the 1910–17 revolution, the Mexican government set out to reclaim the country's Indian past. It emphasized the links between the pre-Hispanic world of the Aztecs and Maya and the modern, largely *mestizo* nation. Government buildings were decorated with murals that celebrated the everyday life of the native peoples.

While the *mestizo* people of the cities have often looked back nostalgically to the country's Indian past and its rich culture, the Indians themselves have often remained second-class citizens. They are usually given the worst land to farm or are forced by poverty to migrate to city slums. In the 1990s, the unrest in Chiapas (see pages 69 and 70) showed that the Indians continued to suffer hardship and discrimination.

Nevertheless, many Indian cultures in Mexico continue to flourish, although this is sometimes because of the rural isolation of their communities. Many ancient Indian languages may have been lost, but some – such as the language of the Aztecs, **Nahuatl** – are still spoken widely and with pride. Here a family of four Tarahumara Indians sits on rocks near the Copper Canyon.

# The economy

*'The theme of the two Mexicos, one developed and the other underdeveloped … is the central theme of our modern history.'*

20th-century Mexican writer Octavio Paz

Today's Mexican economy is a mixture of privately and government-owned industries. Until the 1910 revolution, many businesses in Mexico were owned by foreign companies. In the decades that followed, the Mexican government nationalized many key sectors (areas), notably the oil and petroleum industries.

The nationalization of the oil industry enabled Mexico to build up a powerful industrial base, and today the country is Latin America's second-largest economy after Brazil. Trade agreements, notably with the USA and Canada, have also helped to boost the economy.

Mexico's economy has some serious weaknesses, however. The country is burdened with massive **foreign debt** and high **inflation**. The workforce is not highly educated, Mexico is not a good innovator and the average annual rate of economic growth is just 2.7 per cent of the country's **gross national product** (GNP).

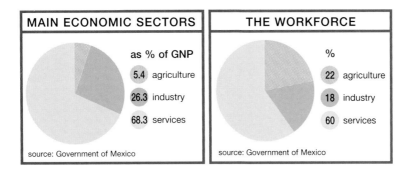

**MAIN ECONOMIC SECTORS**

as % of GNP

5.4 agriculture

26.3 industry

68.3 services

source: Government of Mexico

**THE WORKFORCE**

%

22 agriculture

18 industry

60 services

source: Government of Mexico

*In ancient Mexico, maize was a staple of the mighty Aztec empire. Today, Mexicans continue to grow maize in the fertile lands of central Mexico.*

*This map shows the distribution of land use in Mexico. Much of the landscape is mountainous, desert or dense rainforest and is often unsuitable for agricultural use.*

## PRIMARY SECTORS

For centuries, the economy of the territory today called Mexico depended almost exclusively on agriculture. The Aztec empire was built on maize, which grew abundantly and with comparatively little labour in the fields of the Mexican Valley. It was the Spanish conquerors who began the intensive exploitation of the country's mineral resources, particularly silver, of which Mexico continues to be the world's leading producer.

# HOW MEXICO USES ITS LAND

crop land
forest
pasture
wetlands
desert

%
**39** permanent pastures
**26** forests/woodlands
**12** arable land
**1** permanent crops
**22** other uses

*The pie chart above shows the percentage of Mexico's land given over to various uses.*

Until the 1940s, mining and farming continued to be the mainstays of Mexico's economy. In recent years, however, manufacturing and tourism have expanded rapidly and are now also very important.

### Farming the land

Mexico is a nation of many farmers – about one person in every four works on the land. However, Mexico is not a rich farming country. Only one-eighth of the land can be cultivated for crops; the rest is too mountainous or too dry. Mexico's richest farmland is found on the high southern plateau and on the flat, low-lying strips along the coast. Most soil on the Yucatán Peninsula, in the south-east, is too thin to be fertile.

Before the Mexican Revolution (see pages 64–6), most Mexican peasant farmers worked on **haciendas**, huge estates run by wealthy landowners. After 1917, the state nationalized the land, and peasants worked on shared farms called *ejidos*. In the 1990s, the state allowed poor farmers to buy or rent their land for the first time.

Mexican farms range from tiny plots of land to large estates run by wealthy corporations. Poor farmers own small plots that yield only enough crops to feed their families. In a good year, there will be a small surplus that can be sold at market.

On small farms, the main crops are the basic foods of the Mexican people. Maize, which people have grown in Mexico for 7000 years, is the primary staple. Maize flour is used to make tortillas, the flat bread that most Mexicans eat every day. Poor farmers also grow potatoes,

**In 1999, Mexico was the fourth-largest producer of coffee, the eighth-largest producer of sugar and the ninth-largest producer of fruit in the world.**

*In the poor and largely agricultural state of Chiapas, tobacco is an important cash crop.*

*The maguey agave is a specialized crop that is used to make Mexico's national alcoholic drink – tequila. Tequila takes it name from a town in the state of Jalisco where most of it is made.*

beans and squash. Using old-fashioned methods, many have to farm rocky land that has thin soil, so their crop yields are often low.

Large farming corporations using new equipment and modern methods produce most of Mexico's cash crops (crops that are grown for **export**). The most important crops grown commercially are coffee, maize, wheat, sugar cane, tobacco and oranges.

Commercial farming is based in three main areas: in parts of the dry north, on the central plateau and in the tropical south. In the north and north-west, irrigation projects have transformed dry areas into fertile farm-land. This region produces most of the country's wheat and cotton, as well as alfalfa and soya beans. Winter vegetables and fruits such as melons and tomatoes are grown in irrigated valleys, mainly for the US market.

The high plateau around Guanajuato, in central Mexico, is known as Mexico's bread basket because of the large amount of crops grown there. In the hot, wet lands of the far south and east, farmers grow tropical crops for export. Coffee and sugar cane are the most important, but many kinds of tropical fruits, including oranges, bananas and pineapples, are also grown. Farmers grow vanilla and cacao plants for use in flavouring and chocolate. They also raise sapodilla trees on plantations and tap the bark for its white, sticky sap. This sap, called chicle, is the main ingredient in chewing gum.

## Ranching, forestry and fishing

Cattle ranching (farming) is a major industry in Mexico. The country is one of the world's leading producers of beef cattle and milk. Farmers often graze cattle on land that is too dry for arable farming. In the north, they raise cattle mainly for meat. On lusher pastures further south, farmers rear dairy cattle for their milk.

Forests cover a quarter of the land in Mexico. On the slopes of the Sierra Madre mountains, lumberjacks cut pine and cedar trees for fuel and timber. The tropical

**Chocolate has been made in Mexico since Mayan and Aztec times. The Aztecs used it for a fortifying drink called *tchocoatl*, which was drunk by warriors before going into battle.**

*Fishing people on Mexico's inland lakes use butterfly nets to snare their catch.*

rainforests of the far south and east contain many valuable hardwood trees, including mahogany and cedar. Vast tracts of forest land have been cleared, but many people fear that native plants and animals will be endangered if the tree-felling continues at the present rate.

With thousands of kilometres of coastline, it is not surprising that fishing is an important industry in Mexico. Shrimp is the main catch, and thousands of tonnes of these shellfish are exported every year. Tuna, red snapper, anchovies, sardines and oysters are also caught. In recent years, refrigerated lorries and other modern equipment have helped the fishing industry become more profitable. On inland lakes, fishing people work from dugout canoes with butterfly-shaped nets.

On the southern Pacific coast and in Baja California, fishing is a popular sport among tourists. Large, powerful fish such as swordfish, sailfish and marlin swim in the blue waters, and anglers compete to see who can land the heaviest fish.

## Natural resources

With its vast mineral resources, Mexico is one of the great mining nations of the world. Gold and silver were the first minerals to be mined in Mexico. Silver-mining developed rapidly during the 300-year period of Spanish colonial rule, when huge amounts of silver were shipped to Spain. Some parts of Mexico were so rich in this precious mineral that it was cheaper to shoe horses with silver than with iron brought over from Spain. For centuries, silver dominated the country's economy, and today Mexico is still the world's leading producer.

The largest silver mines are in northern and central Mexico, particularly around Guanajuato and San Luis Potosí. Mexico also has rich deposits of many other minerals, including copper, gold, lead and sulphur. Miners also extract iron ore, mercury, zinc and antimony. Minerals are mainly extracted for export, though some, such as iron, are also used in domestic industries.

**ENERGY SOURCES**

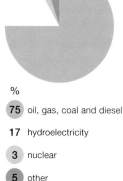

%
75  oil, gas, coal and diesel

17  hydroelectricity

3  nuclear

5  other

source: Government of Mexico

*Mexico relies heavily on its resources of oil and natural gas to meet its energy needs. The government also has a substantial nuclear power programme. Mexico's first nuclear plant was built at Laguna Verde.*

Mexico's natural resources supply most of the country's energy needs and have also given a boost to the development of industry. Oil is Mexico's greatest single asset. It was first discovered in Mexico in about 1900. By the 1920s, Mexico had become one of the world's leading oil producers. In the early years, the oil industry was in the hands of foreign companies, mainly from the UK and the USA. In 1938, however, the Mexican government seized control of the oil industry. Since that time, oil production and refining have been run by a national company, PEMEX – Petroleos Mexicanos.

In the 1970s, vast, new oil fields were discovered along the Gulf Coast and in the ocean bed offshore. The high price of oil brought large profits and helped with the development of manufacturing industry. In the 1980s, though, oil prices fell. Today, oil continues to be vital to the economy, and Mexico ranks about fifth in oil production in the world. Much of Mexico's 'black gold'

*The Gulf of Mexico is dotted with drilling platforms like this one. The oil industry generates much of Mexico's wealth and many of its jobs.*

**Mexico is the ninth-biggest producer of energy and the thirteenth-biggest consumer of energy in the world.**

# Mexico's handicrafts

There is a long tradition in Mexico of making beautiful textiles, ceramics and jewellery. Very often, the vivid colours and striking designs used in these objects can be traced back to pre-Hispanic times. Sometimes, too, designs are copies of Aztec or Mayan originals. For example, chubby pottery dogs, originally made by the ancient inhabitants of western Mexico, are today sold in markets everywhere.

Despite rapid modernization, Mexico still produces a vast amount of handicrafts (*artesanías*). Hardly a tourist visits Mexico without buying an embroidered blouse, a decorated pot or a wall hanging. Selling handicrafts is therefore both an important way of bringing foreign currency into the country and a means for native peoples to generate badly needed income.

Mexico's handicrafts are not simply a way of making money, however. Regional traditional crafts are handed down from generation to generation. Mexicans, like this woman in Chiapas, take genuine pride in the traditions and skills that have gone into their work.

is extracted by the huge drilling platforms that have been erected off the Gulf Coast. While oil is used in local industries, much is exported, mainly to the USA. Mexico also has vast fields of natural gas, notably at Reynosa in north-eastern Mexico and around Veracruz.

The rivers that flow from the central plateau also provide energy for Mexico. These fast-flowing waters have been harnessed to generate hydroelectric power. The most important hydroelectric plants are on the Tonto, Balsas and Grijalva rivers.

Chicoasan Dam on the Balsas River is one of the highest dams in the world. Another large project is planned for the Grijalva. Local Indian groups are protesting against this dam because it will flood villages and ancient sites and destroy wildlife habitats.

## The manufacturing industry

Mexico has one of the most modern manufacturing industries in Latin America. The biggest impetus to industrial development came in March 1938 when President Lázaro Cárdenas nationalized the oil industry, which previously had been in the hands of foreign investors. The new oil company, PEMEX, gave Mexico the capacity to fuel the industrial revolution that followed. Industry was further developed during World War Two (1939–45), when the USA helped set up many factories in Mexico to make the equipment and machinery needed for the US war effort.

Today, Mexican factories are efficient and modern and produce a wide variety of goods. The main products are motor vehicles, chemicals, clothing, cement, steel, iron and processed food and drink. Cheap energy, abundant raw materials and low wages help Mexico compete in the world market of manufactured goods.

Many of Mexico's industries make use of local resources. Iron and coal are used to make steel; cotton is used for clothing. Cement is made from stone, sand and gravel dredged from local quarries.

**Mexicans think of 18 March – the date on which President Cárdenas nationalized the oil industry in 1938 – as the anniversary of their country's economic independence.**

83

# MAJOR INDUSTRIES

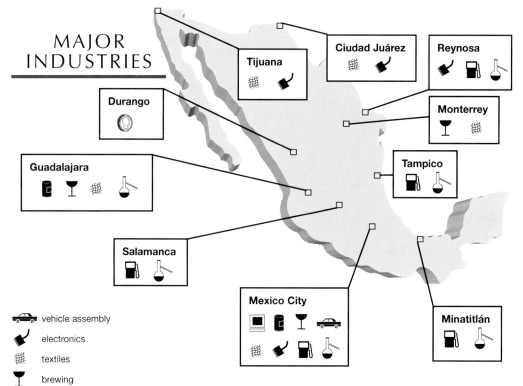

Tijuana

Ciudad Juárez

Reynosa

Durango

Monterrey

Guadalajara

Tampico

Salamanca

Mexico City

Minatitlán

vehicle assembly

electronics

textiles

brewing

computers

petrochemicals

silver mining

food processing

oil and gas

*Mexico is one of
Latin America's
most industrialized
countries. Much
of its industry is
concentrated in small
pockets around major
urban areas such as
Mexico City and
Monterrey.*

Food-processing industries, which form about one-quarter of all manufacturing, make use of many local crops. Drinks made in Mexico, including beer and tequila, are popular all over the world. Beer is made from hops, and tequila is made from the fermented sap of the **maguey agave** (see page 24).

Mexico City is the most important industrial centre in Mexico. The capital and its suburbs produce about half of all goods made in the country. Cars, refrigerators, washing machines and processed foodstuffs are leading products of the region. Guadalajara, Puebla and other large towns of the central plateau also have many modern factories.

In the north-east, Monterrey, Mexico's third-largest city, is another major centre for industry. The discovery of rich deposits of iron ore and coal in the mountains around the city led to the development of the iron and steel industry there. Nowadays, cement, chemicals and clothing are also made in Monterrey. The city's breweries are renowned all over the world.

The strip of land along the border with the USA forms another major industrial region. Assembly plants known as *maquiladoras* have been built here. Factories owned by companies from the USA take advantage of low wages in Mexico to produce goods cheaply. Increasingly, these factories are owned by international Japanese and Mexican corporations.

## The growth of tourism

With so much to do and see in Mexico, it is no wonder that tourism is thriving. More than 19 million tourists visit every year, and eight out of ten visitors come from the USA. The industry brings in large sums of much-needed foreign currency – more than 4500 million pounds each year – and provides jobs for 10 per cent of Mexico's workforce.

Tourists come to sightsee and shop in busy Mexico City or to explore the beautiful colonial cities such as Guadalajara, Guanajuato and San Miguel de Allende. Many tourists go to marvel at the ancient sites, including Teotihuacán and the Mayan ruins of the Yucatán Peninsula. Others enjoy the wonderful beaches and go snorkelling or scuba-diving in the clear, blue seas.

Some of Mexico's most popular resorts are Cancún (see page 86) and Cozumel Island in the Caribbean, Acapulco and Puerto Vallarta on the Pacific coast and Cabo San Lucas in Baja California.

## TRADE: IMPORTS AND EXPORTS

Mexico's main exports reflect its status as a largely industrialized nation. Unlike the countries of Central America, which export mostly agricultural produce, Mexico's chief exports are motor vehicles and parts and oil and oil products. Other major exports include chemicals and minerals, as well as coffee, cotton and electronic goods. The country's chief **imports** are industrial and agricultural machinery, electrical equipment, motor vehicles and aircraft.

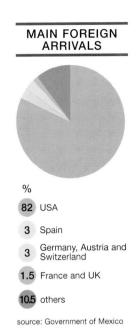

**MAIN FOREIGN ARRIVALS**

%
- 82 USA
- 3 Spain
- 3 Germany, Austria and Switzerland
- 1.5 France and UK
- 10.5 others

source: Government of Mexico

*Most of Mexico's tourists come from the USA. The closeness, beautiful beach resorts and rich archaeological heritage make Mexico an attractive destination for many US citizens.*

# The beach resort of Cancún

During the 1970s, the Mexican government began to invest heavily in the country's tourism industry. Tourism, the government realized, could be used to give a much-needed boost to the economies of remoter areas such as Baja California and the Yucatán Peninsula, providing jobs for local people and bringing in foreign currency.

One area that developers struck upon was the remote and sparsely populated state of Quintana Roo, on the Yucatán Peninsula. However, the region lacked almost everything a tourist region needs – hotels, an airport

or even a major road. The one thing it did have was its natural beauty – kilometres of unspoilt Caribbean coastline, white beaches and tropical forest.

With the government's blessing, developers began to build a string of new resorts along the coast. Of these, Cancún was by far the most ambitious. On a 23-km-long (14-mile) deserted spit of sand stretching out like the number '7' into the Caribbean Sea, dozens of dazzling new hotels were built. A new airport and roads were built on the mainland. In the beginning, too, the area was a duty-free zone, and even today, the sales tax is considerably less than elsewhere in Mexico.

Mexico's main trading partner is the USA. About 84 per cent of Mexico's exports go to its powerful northern neighbour, and 75 per cent of its imports come from there. Other important trade partners are Canada and Japan. In 1993, Mexico signed the North American Free Trade Agreement (NAFTA) with the USA and Canada (see page 69). Over the following fifteen years, NAFTA aimed to create a huge free-trade zone in which the signatories (the signing parties) could trade goods without paying duties. Mexico's membership in NAFTA helped the economy to grow by 3.5 per cent in 1994.

In 1994, however, there was a dramatic fall in the value of the peso, which led to a severe financial crisis in Mexico. A group of countries, led by the USA, lent Mexico financial assistance, which enabled the Mexican economy to recover. In 1996, the economy began to recover, although only slowly. Inflation and unemployment fell, and the peso stabilized. NAFTA helped with Mexico's recovery because it enabled Mexico to increase its exports rather than cut its imports from the USA. Mexico, however, is saddled with a huge foreign debt – currently it is more than 104,000 million pounds.

Mexico also has trade links with the other countries of Latin America as a member of the Latin American Integration Association (LAIA), which promotes regional free trade, and as a member of G3, which aims to remove trade restrictions between Mexico, Colombia and Venezuela.

| EXPORTS (£000 m) | | IMPORTS (£000 m) | |
|---|---|---|---|
| manufactured products | 27.1 | intermediate goods | 44.9 |
| crude oil & products | 7.3 | capital goods | 6.8 |
| agriculture | 2.3 | consumer goods | 4.2 |
| other | 23.3 | | |

source: Government of Mexico

*The charts above show that the value of Mexico's exports exceeds the value of its imports. The charts below show Mexico's major trading partners.*

MAIN TRADING PARTNERS

EXPORTS
% 
83.9 USA
2.3 Canada
1.4 Japan
1.0 Spain
0.8 Switzerland
10.6 others

IMPORTS
%
75.5 USA
4.6 Japan
3.5 Germany
1.9 Canada
1.1 France
13.4 others

## THE TRANSPORTATION SYSTEM

Mexico developed a unified transportation network only slowly, although it was the first Latin American country to build railways. Nevertheless, in the last decades of the 20th century, rail and road connections improved hugely. The capital, Mexico City, is at the hub of these connections. Today, air travel has become an important means of travelling within the country.

### Motorways and other roads

The nation has 88,367 kilometres (54,910 miles) of paved roads and 3166 kilometres (1967 miles) of motorways or major national highways. The mountainous terrain in Mexico makes it far easier to travel between north and south than between east and west. The distances between Mexican cities are often huge, and road travel can be slow. For instance, it can take more than a day to reach the Yucatán Peninsula, in the south-east, or Chiapas, in the far south, from the capital, Mexico City. Drivers travelling east or west through the Sierra Madres must negotiate twisting roads, high, snowy passes and even landslides.

Four major roads link Mexico City to the northern border. The most important is the Pan-American Highway, which in Mexico runs for 1996 kilometres (1240 miles) and links Mexico with seventeen countries.

There are more than 5 million cars in Mexico. Three million of these are in Mexico City, causing traffic congestion and severe pollution. Many people use shared taxis (*peseros*) to get around the capital. Both in large towns and in the countryside, buses are a popular form of transport. They range from luxurious,

## The Pan-American Highway

The Pan-American Highway is the world's longest paved road. It snakes for 26,000 km (16,000 miles) between the US state of Alaska in the far north and Tierra del Fuego in the far south of Argentina. The highway is interrupted only by a swathe of rainforest in Panama. Here the Pan-American comes to a halt and resurfaces 107 km (66 miles) away in Colombia.

The US, Mexican and Colombian governments are eager to bridge this gap – they see the highway as a vital link in an expanded North American Free Trade Agreement (NAFTA).

Tijuana
Mexicali
Ciudad Juárez
Chihuahua
Guaymas
Nuevo Laredo
Monterrey
Matamoros
Torreón
La Paz
Mazatlán
Tampico
Mérida
Cancún
Guadalajara
Mexico City
León
Veracruz
Minatitlán
Cuernavaca
Oaxaca
Acapulco
major road
railway
major airport
ferry crossing

## TRANSPORTATION

Mexico's transportation system has developed massively in recent years. Air travel and the road network have been vastly improved.

air-conditioned coaches to dilapidated bone-shakers that seem to run to no timetable. Out in the countryside, many people use horses, burros (small donkeys) or bicycles to travel over the rough dirt roads. Heavy loads are piled on ox carts or motorbikes, or simply carried on people's backs.

**On Mexico's main roads, the maximum speed is 100 km (62 miles) per hour.**

**On the faster and better-maintained main roads and on motorways, there are tolls (*cuota*) at which car drivers have to pay a fee to use the road.**

### Rail, sea and air

Mexico has more than 26,500 kilometres (16,430 miles) of railways. Much of the rail network dates back to the dictatorship of Porfirio Díaz from 1876 to 1911 (see pages 63–4). In the early 1900s, the railways helped to open up the country. Now they are mostly owned by the government and offer cheap fares and freight rates. They can, however, be uncomfortable and, at worst, unsafe.

Much of the rail network is currently being privatized – that is, sold into private ownership – including the country's main freight line. Most businesses, however, prefer to send their freight by road because they consider the railways to be slow and unreliable.

Owing to the city's altitude, Mexico City's underground (metro) claims to be the highest underground network in the world (see page 31). More than 4 million people use it every day, and trains are packed during rush hours. The cost of underground travel is low because one cheap fare is valid for all destinations.

Mexico's sea ports handle most of its trade with foreign countries. The two main ports are Veracruz and Tampico, both on the Gulf Coast. Other major ports include Guaymas and Salina Cruz, on the Pacific Coast, and Coatzacoalcos, on the Gulf. There are also 2900 kilometres (1802 miles) of navigable waterways.

Air travel allows passengers to reach remote places easily and to cover huge distances far more quickly than they would with any other form of transport. Throughout the world, 30 international airports have flights to Mexico. In Mexico, the main airports are Mexico City, Guadalajara, Acapulco, Monterrey and Mérida. There are two national airlines – Aeroméxico and Mexicana.

## Going to Mexico

Getting to Mexico from the USA is very easy today because the transportation systems of both countries are largely integrated. There are lots of flights available from US cities, but the cheapest are from the southern 'gateway' cities, such as Dallas and Houston.

There are more than twenty border crossings from the USA into Mexico. At the border, officials issue all passport-bearing visitors with a tourist card. This entitles them to stay in Mexico for up to 90 days or longer if they can show that they have the means to support themselves. Mexico, like many other countries, is concerned about illegal immigrants.

There is also a so-called free zone (*zona libre*) that stretches for about 24 kilometres (15 miles) south of the US border, where it is possible for visitors to stay for up to three days without having first gone through immigration control.

- With about 26,500 km (16,430 miles) of track, Mexico has the eighth-longest railway network in the world.

- There are 45 vehicles per km of road in Mexico, compared with 62 vehicles per km in the UK.

- Some border crossings between Mexico and the USA are open 24 hours a day.

# The Mexican railways

After a promising beginning under the presidency of Porfirio Díaz at the end of the 19th century, Mexico's nationally owned railway system (*Ferrocarriles Nacionales de México*) now has a very poor reputation. Today, trains are famous not only for their cheapness but also for their slowness. For example, it can take up to 42 hours to go by train from Mexico City to Mérida, in the Yucatán. Sometimes a train can be hours late, or not even turn up at all! No wonder many Mexicans prefer to catch a plane.

If, however, you want to travel at your ease through some of the Americas' most spectacular scenery, then the railway can be a good option. One of the most famous railways runs through the Copper Canyon (below).

The government is trying to improve matters. There are fast new intercity trains running out of Mexico City, and there are plans to sell off the railway to private investors. Private companies are unlikely to run the badly needed services in remoter regions, though.

# Arts and living

*'Let us, for our part, go back to the work of the ancient inhabitants of our valleys, the Indian painters and sculptors …'*

Mexican painter David A. Siqueiros (1896–1974)

Mexico's rich artistic culture stretches back to ancient times. Highly advanced cultures existed in Mexico long before the Spanish conquerors arrived in the 16th century. Despite the devastation inflicted on their artistic heritage by the Spanish conquistadors, much of the ancient Indians' astonishing art survives today and can be seen in museums throughout Mexico and around the world.

The art of the ancient civilizations survived in another way, too. After the conquest, there was a great deal of continuity between the art of the pre-Hispanic world and that of the new colony. Painters and architects took up the styles of European artists, but at the same time often gave them a strongly Mexican look.

Local materials, such as the reddish-brown *tezontle* stone, the traditional techniques and tastes of the native craftsworkers and the sunny, colourful environment of Mexico itself all helped to shape a distinctive 'Mexican' culture. By the time of the Mexican Revolution, artists took great pride in the 'Mexicanness' of their work.

The same continuity between pre-Hispanic and Hispanic Mexico can be seen in everyday life. Even within the large, cosmopolitan cities, Mexico's largely *mestizo* people eat, drink, dance and sing in an unmistakably Mexican way. Many Indian peoples, of course, continue to live traditional lives.

**The 20th-century church of Our Lady of Guadalupe in Puerto Vallarta is famous for its crown-shaped tower overlooking the Pacific Ocean.**

## FACT FILE

● The art of mural (wall) painting stretches at least as far back as the civilization of Teotihuacán, where painters used bright colours to decorate the temple walls. The art was revived in the 20th century by Diego Rivera, José Orozco and David Sequeiros.

● In the early 20th century, the term *'indigenismo'* (Indianism) was used to refer to art that took inspiration from the culture of ancient Mexico.

● In the early 20th century, many non-Mexican writers and artists came to Mexico for inspiration, among them the famous British writer D. H. Lawrence.

## THE ARTS

Mexican painters and writers have won a worldwide reputation for the forceful originality of their work. They have managed to straddle both Old and New worlds, looking back to both the traditional folk arts of their country and the innovations of artists in Europe and the USA.

*Below is a plan of a typical stepped Mayan pyramid-temple. Broad flights of stairs led to the summit of the temple.*

### From pyramids to skyscrapers

Mexico's first architects were the **Toltecs**, **Aztecs** and **Maya**, who designed vast temple complexes and elaborate palaces. Many of these sacred buildings took the form of flat-topped, stone pyramids. Mexico's three greatest pyramids are the Pyramid of the Sun and the Pyramid of the Moon at Teotihuacán (see page 48) and the Great Pyramid at Cholula near Puebla (see page 43). Such temples were often crowned with a simple shrine.

The Aztecs tended to erect buildings that were awe-inspiring because of their vast size. The Maya, by contrast, created elaborately shaped and decorated temples and palaces. Such decorations included sculptures of jaguars, eagles devouring human hearts and feathered serpents. Columns were made in the shape of warriors, and temples were guarded by reclining figures called *chacmools* (see page 44).

The word 'Churrigueresque' derives from the name of the Spanish carver and architect José Benito de Churriguera who helped to develop this style.

In colonial times, the Spanish built numerous graceful churches, often with the help of Indian workers. The facades and doorways of these early churches were often decorated in a style known as plateresque. This term was from the Spanish word '*platero*', meaning 'silversmith,' because the style resembled the intricate ornamental silverwork made at that time. Later churches were often built in an even more extravagant style known as Churrigueresque (see panel left).

The great cathedrals of such cities as Mexico City and Guadalajara took many generations to build, and display a mixture of many different styles of architecture.

Their outside walls are covered with stone carvings, and their interiors are filled with paintings, sculptures and altarpieces decorated with gold leaf. In and around Puebla, churches were often decorated with colourful glazed tiles known as *azulejos* (see page 43).

In recent times, modern architects have designed many impressive buildings. One of the most famous is the National Museum of Anthropology, designed by Pedro Ramírez Vazquez. This building blends ancient Indian design with modern building techniques.

*Even the everyday architecture of Mexico shows its people's love of colour – reds, oranges, corn yellow and azure blue.*

## Wall paintings

Mexico's most famous paintings are its murals (wall paintings). The art of mural painting dates back to the Mayas and continued during the colonial period, when churches were decorated with religious frescoes (murals painted on wet plaster).

Mexico's best-known murals, however, were painted just after the Mexican Revolution (1910–20). From the 1920s, revolutionary artists covered the walls of many public buildings with political scenes or events from history. The most famous muralists are Diego Rivera

**The idea for the revolutionary murals came from the education minister, José Vasconcelos. He wanted to promote awareness of Mexican history.**

# Frida Kahlo

Frida Kahlo (1907–54) is one of Mexico's most popular artists. Her intense, brilliantly coloured self-portraits can be found in almost every major gallery in the world. Her striking looks, with glossy black hair and bushy eyebrows, and agonized but dignified stare, create an unforgettable image.

Kahlo's deeply personal art was shaped by her tragic, stormy life. She was born in the town of Coyoacán, part of the southern sprawl of Mexico City. At the age of sixteen, Kahlo suffered terrible spinal injuries in a trolley-car accident. During her long, painful recovery, she taught herself to paint.

Kahlo also became acquainted with the mural painter Diego Rivera, who admired her painting. In 1929, the two artists married and went to live together in Kahlo's family home. Their relationship was always difficult, and at one stage, the couple divorced – only to marry again two years later.

For much of her life, Kahlo used a wheelchair and was sometimes confined to a hospital bed. She made herself the principal subject of her art. Her self-portraits showed the pain and vulnerability of her body, and her struggle to understand her relationship with Rivera and with her *mestizo* roots. In this picture, called *Diego and I*, she showed how much she felt Rivera to be a part of her by painting his portrait on her forehead.

After Kahlo's death, her home in Coyoacán became a museum devoted to her art. It houses not only her extraordinary paintings and photographs of her and Rivera but also a wonderful collection of the Mexican folk art that inspired her.

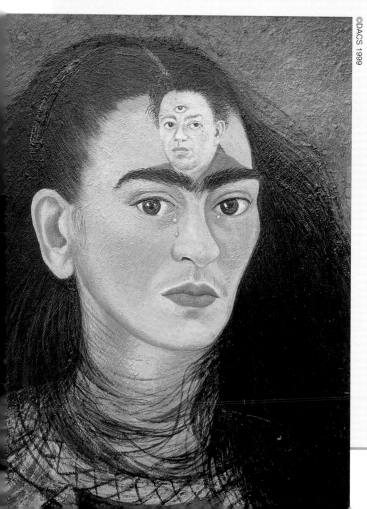

©DACS 1999

(1886–1957), David Alfaro Siqueiros (1896–1974) and José Clemente Orozco (1883–1949). Diego Rivera was the founder of the movement. Many of his most famous works show the Indian way of life before the Spanish conquest and scenes from Mexican history (see page 33). Many of his murals can be seen in the Palacio Nacional (National Palace) in Mexico City.

Siqueiros fought in the Mexican Revolution under Venustiano Carranza. His monumental murals, found in many government buildings throughout Mexico, reflect his ardent faith in communism. José Clemente Orozco was a passionate artist whose most famous works are the murals for the Hospicio Cabañas in Guadalajara. These include a powerful portrait of Miguel Hidalgo, the father of Mexican independence (see page 57).

Rufino Tamayo (1899–1991) was a native Zapotec artist who worked in the same tradition. His paintings are a blend of Indian art and cubism, a contemporary European art movement that depicted reality in fragments. Frida Kahlo is one of Mexico's finest artists, painting brilliantly coloured self-portraits in a blend of Indian and European styles (see box opposite).

## Poetry and novels

Mexico's literary heritage also dates back to precolonial times. The ancient peoples of Mexico produced poetry and other sacred writings, but unfortunately many manuscripts were destroyed. Netza-hualcoyotl (*Net-sah-hoo-al-coy-ot-ul*), king of Texcoco in the 15th century, was renowned as a poet. The poems sung at his court survive today.

Later, in the 17th century, a learned nun called Sor (Sister) Juana Inés de la Cruz (1651–95) wrote poems that are

Rivera and Orozco also painted murals in the USA. These include examples in the Rockefeller Center in New York and the San Francisco Stock Exchange. In the UK, the Tate Gallery in London has paintings by Rivera in its collection.

## An Aztec poem

A king of the city of Texcoco, Netzahualcoyotl, wrote this poem just before the Spanish conquest. It is full of gloomy foreboding.

*Just as a painting*
*We will be dimmed.*
*Just as a flower*
*We shall wither.*
*Think of this,*
*Eagle and Jaguar knights,*
*Though you were carved in jade*
*Though you were made of gold,*
*You will also go there*
*To the land of the fleshless.*
*We must all vanish,*
*None may remain.*

among the finest in the Spanish language. Sor Juana had an interest in science and politics and was a forward-looking thinker for her time.

In the early 19th century, José Fernández de Lizardi (1776–1827) wrote the first Latin American novel, *The Mangy Parrot*, which poked fun at the society of his day. During the 20th century, Mexico produced many great writers. Juan Rulfo (1918– 86) pioneered the school of novel writing called magic realism, while Octavio Paz (1914–98) was a poet and essay writer. The latter's most famous work is *Labyrinth of Solitude* in which he wrote about the Mexican character. In 1990, Paz won the Nobel Prize for Literature. Carlos Fuentes (born 1928) is Mexico's best-known writer. He has written more than a dozen novels, including his famous book about Mexico, *Where the Air Is Clear*.

## Music and dance

In ancient times, Indian peoples made music with wooden flutes and sea shells, gourd rattles and drums. Recently, there has been a revival of this music, and modern musicians are using traditional instruments.

*In village fiestas throughout Mexico, large bands of musicians provide the entertainment. The fiesta style of music usually features brass, drums and the occasional guitar.*

Mexico is probably most famous for its *mariachi* music, which dates back to the 18th century. Bands of these strolling musicians perform throughout Mexico, dressed in cowboy costume. The singers deliver passionate love songs accompanied by trumpets, violins and guitars. The country is also well known for its marimba bands. Marimba players strike their wooden instruments with rubber-tipped sticks.

No Mexican fiesta (festival) would be complete without folk dancing as well as music. The most famous dance is the *jarabe tapatio* – the Mexican hat dance.

Male dancers dress in dashing cowboy outfits. Women wear the national costume, called *china poblana*, which is a full red-and-green skirt, embroidered blouse and brightly coloured sash. This outfit is named after an Asian princess who arrived in Mexico as a slave (see page 42).

The best-known dance company in Mexico is the Ballet Folklórico de México. This was founded in 1952 by the dancer Amalia Hernández, and performs regularly at the Palace of Fine Arts in Mexico City. The performances are a colourful, vibrant whirl of coloured lights, traditional costumes and music and dance from all over Mexico.

## The Voladores dance

The extraordinary Voladores (Fliers) dance dates back to before Aztec times, when it may have been a religious rite. Five men climb up to a platform on top of a tall pole. While one plays on a flute or a drum, the others tie ropes, coiled around the top of the pole, to their waists. They then fling themselves off the platform and spiral downwards to the ground and – usually – a safe landing. Each man turns round the pole thirteen times, making 52 turns in all. This number symbolizes the 52-year cycle of the ancient Mesoamerican calendar (see page 47).

## FIESTA TIME!

Mexico is famous for its colourful fiestas. Some of these celebrate national holidays and important dates in Mexico's history. Many mark saints' feast days in the religious year. Fiestas usually begin at dawn with a shower of fireworks and the tolling of church bells. Many people wear Indian costumes or *charro* (cowboy) outfits and parade through the streets to the sound of *mariachi* bands. Churches are decked with flowers, and people go in to light a candle and say a special prayer.

On 16 September, Independence Day is marked by fiestas all over Mexico. The main celebration takes place in Mexico City. On the eve of Independence Day, a huge crowd gathers in the **Zócalo** (main square) to hear the president recite the Grito de Dolores (see page 57), the famous speech that heralded the struggle for independence. Celebrations continue the next day, with fireworks, dancing and horseracing. There are also celebrations on 5 May – Cinco de Mayo – to commemorate the defeat of the French at Puebla in 1862.

One of the greatest fiestas is held on 12 December in honour of Our Lady of Guadalupe (that is, the Virgin Mary), the patron saint of Mexico. This festival marks the anniversary of the day in 1531 when the Virgin Mary is believed to have appeared to Juan Diego, an Indian peasant, on Tepeyac Hill in Mex- ico City. Soon after this fiesta comes Christmas, when there are nine days of processions, called *posadas*. These processions act out Joseph and

## National holidays and festivals

| | |
|---|---|
| 1 January | New Year's Day |
| 6 January | Epiphany |
| 5 February | Constitution Day |
| 21 March | Birthday of Benito Juárez |
| March/April | Holy Week and Easter |
| 1 May | Labour Day |
| 5 May | Battle of Puebla |
| 10 May | Mother's Day |
| 1 September | President's State of the Union Message |
| 16 September | Independence Day |
| 12 October | Columbus Day |
| 2 November | Day of the Dead |
| 20 November | Revolution Day |
| 12 December | Homage to Our Lady of Guadalupe |
| 16–24 December | *posadas* |
| 25 December | Christmas Day |

Mary's journey to Bethlehem and their search for room at the inn. After each *posada*, clay or papier-mâché pots filled with toys and sweets, called *piñatas*, are hung high above the ground. Blindfolded children take turns trying to break open the pots with a long pole. When the *piñata* breaks, the children scramble for the scattered gifts.

The Day of the Dead, on 2 November, is one of Mexico's most famous festivals. On this day, people remember friends and relatives who have died. Each family puts on a lavish banquet decorated with flowers, and people light incense and candles to guide the spirits of dead relatives to the feast. People also carry offerings of food and flowers to family graves. Once the spirits are thought to have had their fill, everyone begins to feast and the celebrations begin. Children exchange choco-late skulls or sweets in the shape of human skeletons.

In late February or early March, the city of Veracruz on Mexico's Gulf Coast erupts with music, dance and fireworks. This explosion of colour and fun is traditionally the final festivity before the 40-day penance of Lent.

# How to say ...

The Mexican people have a well-earned reputation for being polite. For them, politeness is a sign of mutual respect. They are always careful to say 'please' and 'thank you' and to smile when they do so.

Many Mexicans speak English, but in every country, people are pleased when a foreigner tries to speak a few words of their language – however falteringly. Below are a few Spanish words and phrases that may be useful should you ever visit Mexico. A rough pronunciation follows in parentheses.

Please   *Por favór* (po-RR fa-VORR)

Thank you   *Gracias* (GRA-see-as)

Yes   *Sí* (SEE)

No   *No* (NO)

Hello   *Ola* (O-la)

Goodbye   *Adiós* (a-dee-OS)

See you later   *Hasta luego* (AST-a loo-AY-go)

Good morning   *Buenos días* (bu-AY-nos DEE-as)

Good afternoon   *Buenas tardes* (bu-AY-nas TARR-des)

Good night   *Buenas noches* (bu-AY-nas NOT-ches)

How are you?   *¿Qué tal?* (KAY TAL)

Sorry   *Lo siento* (LO see-EN-toe)

Excuse me   *Con permiso* (con per-MEES-o)

I understand   *Entiendo* (en-tee-EN-doe)

I don't understand   *No entiendo* (NOE en-tee-EN-doe)

Do you speak English?   *¿Habla inglés?* (ab-la ing-LAYSS)

You're welcome   *De nada* (day NA-da)

What is your name?   *¿Como se llama usted?* (COM-o say ya-ma oos-TED)

My name is...   *Me llamo...* (may YA-mo)

Sir/Mr   *Señor* (say-NYORR)

Madam/Mrs   *Señora* (say-NYOR-ra)

Miss   *Señorita* (say-nyo-REE-ta)

**Numbers:**

One/a   *Un/una/uno* (OON/OO-na/OO-no)

Two   *Dos* (DOSS)

Three   *Tres* (TRESS)

Four   *Cuatro* (KWA-tro)

Five   *Cinco* (SINK-o)

Six   *Seis* (SAY-iss)

Seven   *Siete* (see-AY-tay)

Eight   *Ocho* (O-cho)

Nine   *Nueve* (noo-EV-ay)

Ten   *Diez* (dee-ESS)

**Days of the week:**

Monday   *Lunes* (LOON-es)

Tuesday   *Martes* (MARR-tes)

Wednesday   *Miercoles* (mee-ERR-co-les)

Thursday   *Jueves* (HWE-bes)

Friday   *Viernes* (vee-ERR-nes)

Saturday   *Sábado* (SA-ba-doe)

Sunday   *Domingo* (doe-MIN-go)

## EVERYDAY LIFE

Life in the city and in the country are very different from each other in Mexico. In the city, the pace of life is often fast and furious. In the country, the way of life is more traditional and the pace is slow.

### Town and country

Many villages in Mexico are built around a central square (*zócalo*). The church stands on the square, and sometimes there are shops or public buildings. Country houses are built of adobe (sundried brick), stone or cement. They may be roofed with tiles or with corrugated iron or thatched with straw. These homes are not strong enough to stand up to the storms and earth tremors that strike Mexico from time to time.

Most country people are farmers who work a small plot of land on steep, stony ground. Poor farmers use old-fashioned farming methods, and most have only a hoe to work the soil. Some farmers own a primitive plough and a horse to pull it. With such simple tools, the work is back-breaking and the hours are long. To earn extra money, the men may help out on building projects or spend their free time trying their luck at the local silver or coal mine.

Market day is a busy time in country areas. Everyone brings food, handwoven clothes or toys to sell or trade. Wares are laid out on cloths spread on the ground in the open air. Market day is a social occasion for the whole community. It is the time to catch up on the latest gossip as well as to haggle over prices.

Nowadays in large towns and cities throughout Mexico, people wear mostly Western-style clothing, such as jeans and T-shirts. In the countryside, clothing is much more traditional. Women wear loose skirts and blouses and cover their head with a *rebozo* (shawl). Men wear cotton shirts and trousers, leather sandals called *huaraches* and sombreros (wide-brimmed hats) to keep the sun off.

*Mexicans spend a large proportion of their income on their daily needs of food, drink and shelter.*

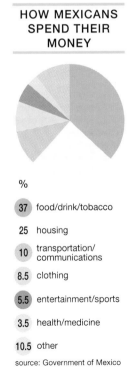

**HOW MEXICANS SPEND THEIR MONEY**

%
- **37** food/drink/tobacco
- **25** housing
- **10** transportation/communications
- **8.5** clothing
- **5.5** entertainment/sports
- **3.5** health/medicine
- **10.5** other

source: Government of Mexico

In cold or rainy weather, men put on a poncho – a square of warm material with a hole in the middle for the head – or wrap a blanket called a *serape* round their shoulders. Shawls, ponchos and blankets are all handwoven in bright colours.

## Wealth and poverty

The cities and large towns of Mexico are home both to great wealth and poverty. In modern city centres, you will find gleaming skyscrapers and glittering shops. But a short bus ride from the centre lie congested sub-urbs and poor shanty towns. In the suburbs, new housing is sometimes cheap and conditions are crowded. But things are even worse in the slums, or 'lost cities', that have sprung up on the outskirts of the largest towns. Here, people build makeshift homes of corrugated iron and scraps of wood or plastic. There is often no electricity or running water and disease is rife.

In 1950, nearly 60 per cent of Mexico's people lived in the country, with just over 40 per cent in towns and cities. Today, only a quarter of the population remains in the country, with nearly three-quarters living in urban areas (see page 9). Mexico's four largest cities are home to about 45 per cent of the population.

*A visit to the market in a Mexicam town or village is a feast for all the senses. Here an Indian woman has spread out her produce – including dark, ripe avocados, herbs and bright green cactus leaves.*

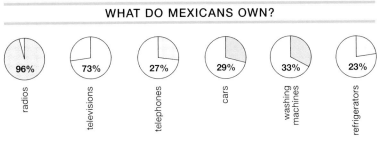

## WHAT DO MEXICANS OWN?

96% radios

73% televisions

27% telephones

29% cars

33% washing machines

23% refrigerators

source: Government of Mexico

*Each chart shows the proportion of Mexican households that own a particular consumer item. While the vast majority of homes have televisions and radios, less than a quarter have refrigerators.*

Every year, about 700,000 people leave the countryside to seek work and a better life in the city, but most newcomers find it very difficult to find work. For men, there are few jobs in the factories. Women may earn a little money doing domestic work such as cleaning. Instead of going to school, the children of these poor families try to make a little money on the streets by cleaning cars or selling chewing gum.

Some families beg or steal to buy enough food to live, or they become involved in the illegal drugs trade. In Mexico City and other major towns, about one in every five families is moderately prosperous. Everyone else lives on or below the poverty line.

In smaller towns, life is a little more comfortable. Work may be easier to find, though many people need two or even three jobs to earn their living. The new suburbs of such towns are usually well laid out and more spacious than those of major cities. Older houses have balconies and a patio or central courtyard, which are often bright with flowers and small shrubs. They are often painted in bright, vibrant colours.

**There is an acute shortage of housing in Mexico. In the Nezahualcóyotl suburb of Mexico City, more than a million people live in shacks.**

## The family

The family is the centre of daily life in Mexico. Many households have between six and ten members. Grandparents often live with their families and look after the grandchildren while the parents are out working. Unmarried adult children often stay on at home, especially young women.

Mealtimes are important occasions when the whole family comes together. For this reason, even small homes have a separate dining room. People celebrate special occasions such as birthdays with lavish feasts and large parties for their friends and relatives.

## Food and drink

Mexican cooking is a distinctive blend of Indian and Spanish styles and is popular all over the world. The most important foods are maize, beans and chilli. Maize is ground into a fine meal and used to make flat bread called tortillas. Tortillas were made in ancient times – there are many Aztec and Mayan sculptures that show people busy making these tasty staples.

Mexicans eat tortillas either plain or filled with meat, chicken, cheese, beans or chilli peppers. When folded and fried, the filled tortillas are known as tacos; rolled up and covered with hot chilli sauce, they are called enchiladas. *Tostadas* are fried until they are crispy, then served flat with a topping. In city streets, there are often *taquerías* – stands selling ready-to-eat tacos.

The Mexican people are very fond of chilli peppers. There are more than a hundred varieties grown, ranging in colour from green to red and black. Not all of them are hot, though the most

*Red* jalapeños *chilli peppers are hung out to dry in the hot sun. Mexicans like to add fiery chillis to their salsas – delicious sauces that are served with almost every meal.*

# Guacamole

Guacamole is a well-known Mexican dish made with avocados. It makes a delicious dip for spicy tortilla chips.

**You will need:** 2 large, ripe avocados, 1 clove garlic, Tabasco sauce, 1/4 lemon or lime, salt and pepper.

**Method:** Cut the avocados in half and remove the stones. Scoop out the flesh with a spoon and put it into a mixing bowl. Mash the avocados with a fork until the mixture is fairly smooth. Peel the garlic and crush it with a knife or garlic-crusher. Add it to the mixture with a dash of Tabasco sauce. Squeeze the lemon or lime into the bowl. Now add salt and pepper to taste, and your dip is ready. Guacamole is best served soon after you make it because it will turn brown if it is left too long.

common variety, the *jalapeño* pepper, certainly is. Tabasco is a hot chilli sauce that is named after the state in south-east Mexico where it was invented.

Beans are often boiled, mashed and then fried. On feast days and celebrations, turkey or chicken is served with *mole*, a rich, brown sauce containing unsweetened chocolate, chillis and spices.

Traditionally, Mexicans eat three meals a day: a simple breakfast, a large lunch and a light supper. Breakfast usually consists of just coffee and a sweet roll (*pan dulce*). At lunchtime, workers in the city often eat a set meal at a restaurant.

The food may be washed down with *agua fresca* – a refreshing blend of fruit juice, sugar and water – or with wine or beer. Hot drinks include strong, sweet coffee and chocolate flavoured with vanilla and cinnamon. When strong liquor is desired, tequila and mescal are

The drink tequila gets its name from a town that lies 50 km (30 miles) north-west of Guadalajara. The drink has been made in the town since the 17th century.

national favourites. Both are made from the fermented sap of **agave** cacti (see page 24). Beer, too, is popular. The most popular brands come from Monterrey, where beer has been brewed since the late 19th century.

## Education for all?

From colonial times until the early 1900s, Mexican schools were run by the Roman Catholic Church. After the Mexican Revolution, the government took charge of education, and from the 1920s, it began opening thousands of schools. Today, education is still a top priority for the government.

In Mexico, all children between the ages of six and fourteen have to go to school by law. Education is free, though parents pay for uniforms and some books. After leaving playschool at the age of six, children go to primary

*A typical schoolroom in Mexico. The government places a high value on education and spends about 10 per cent of its annual budget on schools and educational equipment, such as computers.*

school until they are twelve. Primary school is followed by three years of basic secondary education and three years of upper secondary if parents can afford it.

Ninety-nine per cent of children attend primary school, but only 53 per cent attend secondary school. Many poorer children leave before the secondary stage to find work that will bring in extra money for their families. In rural areas, where schooling is often not as good as in the towns and cities, classes include radio or TV broadcasts that cover the national curriculum.

Mexico has more than 2000 centres for higher education, including universities, training colleges and technical institutes. Courses last between three and seven years. Mexico's oldest university is the National Autonomous University of Mexico in Mexico City. It was founded by the Spanish in 1551. About 15 per cent of the population aged twenty to 24 enroll in a higher-education institution.

## A nation's health

In 1960, the average life expectancy in Mexico was 55. Nowadays, improved health care and better sanitation (disposal of waste and sewage) in the cities have helped people to live longer, and the average life expectancy is 73 years. This is comparable with the UK, where the average life expectancy is 78, and is higher than in most Latin American countries.

The government is in charge of health care and helps pay for treatment. Generally, however, health care is very basic. For people without work, there is very little care at all. Private care is available for those who can afford it.

Health services are generally better in towns than in the country. In rural areas, clinics offer a very basic service, so people must travel to towns for specialist treatment. In large cities, the rising population puts pressure on health services that are already stretched. The major causes of death in Mexico are heart disease, accidents, cancer, violence and tuberculosis.

**EDUCATIONAL ATTENDANCE**

higher education    15%

secondary school    53%

primary school    99%

*While almost every Mexican child goes to primary school, attendance at secondary school is low. This fact is of great concern to the Mexican government, which realizes that the future success of Mexico's economy will depend to a large extent on a well-educated workforce.*

## Sport: from football to bullfighting

Mexico's sports and leisure activities reflect its Indian and Spanish heritage, as well as the influence of the USA. Football (*fútbol*) is the single most popular sport in Mexico. Every small town has its own football team, and large towns and cities may boast at least a couple of professional teams.

There is a fiercely contested first division (*primera división*) of twenty teams. The two most popular teams are América, based in Mexico City and nicknamed Las Águilas (The Eagles), and Guadalajara, nicknamed Las Chivas (The Goats). The biggest matches in Mexico are those between these two teams and are nicknamed los Classicos. The matches are played in Mexico City's Estadio Azteca (Aztec Stadium), which can seat up to 108,500 people. The games are very lively but generally good-humoured.

Children begin to kick a ball as soon as they can walk, and football is played by girls as well as boys. Mexico has hosted the World Cup twice, in 1970 and 1986, but has yet to win football's most sought-after trophy. The national team has a huge, devoted following.

Basketball is another loved sport. The ancient Maya played their own version of the game (see page 47) long before the Spanish conquest. Today, international sports such as volleyball and tennis are also popular. Baseball (*beisbol*) is another popular sport, and watersports, such as snorkelling and diving, are enjoyed on the coast, particularly in Baja California and the Yucatán Peninsula.

## Lucha libre

After football, the most popular spectator sport in Mexico is *lucha libre* (masked wrestling). In Mexico City, there are fights almost every night of the week, and the big bouts are always shown on TV. Traditionally, the wrestlers wear masks to keep their identity secret.

Mexican wrestling is even faster and more aggressive than the kind found in the UK, and the moves are more complicated. Often, too, there are more than two wrestlers in the ring at one time. The wrestlers play up to the audience. A 'baddie' (*rudo*) uses sneaky tricks to foil his opponent, while the 'goodie' (*téchnico*) always plays fair and square.

Many Mexicans love to discuss their favourite wrestlers, and there are magazines and films devoted to the sport. The most famous wrestler was El Santo, who also starred in popular wrestling films.

The Spanish brought bullfighting (*corrida de toros*) to Mexico. On Sundays, people flock to the bullring to watch dashing matadors and mounted picadors armed with long lances show off their skills. First, the picadors enter the ring and weaken the bull by striking repeatedly at his shoulder muscles. Then another group of men enter the ring on foot. These are the *banderilleros*, bullfighters armed with darts 1 metre (3 feet) long. The *banderilleros* have to get three such darts into the bull's shoulders without being gored.

Finally the star of the show enters – the matador. He has exactly sixteen minutes to kill the bull, baiting it with his cape and finally dealing it what he hopes will be a death-blow between the shoulders. Sometimes, if a bull fights courageously, its life is spared. As many as six bulls may be fought during one afternoon. Mexico City has the biggest bullring in the world, seating 55,000 people.

Cockfighting, which is against the law in many countries, is legal in Mexico. Spectators bet large sums on strong-looking birds.

*A referee intervenes after a masked wrestler has forced his opponent to the ground during a lucha libre match.*

**The audience at a bullfight judges how well the matador has fought. If he has fought well, he is awarded one or both of the bull's ears. If his performance has been outstanding, he is awarded the tail as well.**

The fast, exciting game of **jai alai** (*frontón*) comes from the Basque region of Spain. Like squash, it is played on a walled court. Players catch and hurl a hard, rubber ball against the walls using a curved basket attached to their arms. Spectators gather to watch the action and bet on the result.

*Charreadas* are Mexican rodeos. At these events, *charros* (cowboys) display their riding skills. The *charros* wear fancy cowboy outfits: short jackets and tight trousers with shiny buttons, wide-brimmed sombreros, floppy bow ties and boots with spurs. There are contests for lassoing, branding and bareback riding. Folk dancers and *mariachi* (street) bands (see page 98) provide a carnival atmosphere.

### Free time

In their leisure time, Mexicans may play their favourite sport or relax around the radio or television. The most popular TV programmes are soap operas. Many programmes come from the USA and are simply dubbed into Spanish.

Every small village has its football pitch and often a basketball court. Large towns have more facilities, including cinemas, video arcades and swimming pools. At weekends, families may enjoy a stroll or a picnic in the park, or take a trip to the beach if they live near the coast.

Mexicans may take their holidays in palm-thatched huts called cabanas on a beach. Sometimes, they simply rent a hammock and hang it up under a palm roof. Otherwise, they may rent a room in one of Mexico's numerous clean and comfortable hotels. Rich Mexicans may take their holidays overseas.

## Mexico's newspapers

Mexico has more than 270 newspapers. The most famous is Mexico City's *Excélsior*, which is read throughout Latin America. Mexico's constitution ensures both freedom of speech and freedom of the press, so that in theory people can write what they like in newspapers as long as it is truthful. In reality, however, governments have kept a tight grip on what newspapers can and cannot print. Criticism of the president is rare, and sometimes, it is said, the government pays newspapers to print flattering stories on their front pages.

# Religion

From the first days of the Spanish conquest, the Roman Catholic Church played a powerful role in organizing the country. It provided education and health care and gave charity to the poor. For this reason, the Church was also a potent unifying force in Mexico; almost everyone – Indians, *mestizos* and whites – belonged.

Religion plays an important role in everyday life in Mexico. There is no official religion, but the vast majority of people are Roman Catholic, following the faith the Spanish brought to the country. Mexicans take their religion very seriously. Most people go to church regularly, and even poor families celebrate occasions such as marriages and baptisms in style. The picture shows penitents on an Easter pilgrimage in Oaxaca. They wear purple hoods and robes to show their sorrow for their sins.

Each town and village has its patron saint. Saints' feast days are celebrated with fiestas. Mexicans particularly venerate Our Lady of Guadalupe, who is Mexico's patron saint. Statues and paintings of the Virgin show her with the dark skin of a *mestizo* Mexican. The Virgin is a powerful, unifying symbol of Mexico's population.

In some parts of Mexico, Indian groups follow their ancient religions and worship the spirits of nature. Very often,

traditional beliefs exist side by side with Christian ones. The Huichol Indians, for instance, who live in the state of Jalisco, worship two Christs together with a goddess called Nakawé. Some old gods are still venerated as 'saints', and many of Mexico's traditions, such as the Voladores dance (see page 99), have their origins in ancient Indian ceremonies.

# The future

*'Poor Mexico – so far from God,
so close to the United States.'*

Mexican president Porfirio Díaz

In 1900, Mexico was a largely undeveloped country, and its economy was based on farming and mining. Today, it is one of the leading industrial nations of Latin America. With many natural resources, Mexico has enormous potential for growth and wealth.

However, the country faces many important problems: high unemployment and **inflation**, large **foreign debts**, overcrowded cities and a growing gulf between rich and poor people. In the 21st century, Mexico must tackle these problems if it is to take its place as one of the great trading nations of the world.

## ECONOMY AND INDUSTRY

Mexico's greatest assets are its natural resources. The country's vast reserves of oil, natural gas and coal have the potential to bring in great wealth, as well as to provide cost-effective energy for national industries. Minerals, including silver, gold and copper, will continue to bring in cash from abroad. And with vast areas of forest and abundant fish in coastal waters, logging and fishing could also develop into major industries.

Mexico's natural beauty and rich history and culture are also great strengths. Every year, millions of people visit Mexico, and the tourist industry brings in large amounts of foreign currency. In recent years, the government has invested heavily in tourism, and there

*These bold skyscrapers in Mexico City's financial district reflect Mexico's confidence in its future as a member of the world's financial community.*

## FACT FILE

- The gap between rich and poor in Mexico is getting bigger – 16% of the population lives in extreme poverty.

- The quality of Mexico's environment is in rapid decline. Overpopulation, pollution and deforestation are just some of the problems.

- Mexico has a wealth of untapped resources. At present, Mexico exploits only about 5% of its mineral resources, making it potentially an extremely powerful economy.

- Mexico has the second-largest economy in Latin America after Brazil.

# Good neighbours?

In about 1900, the dictator Porfirio Díaz summed up Mexico's relations with the USA thus: 'Poor Mexico! So far from God and so close to the United States.' Díaz meant to draw attention to the mixed blessings that Mexico's closeness to the mighty USA brought. Today, Mexico's relationship with its northern neighbour continues to trouble the people of both nations.

In the 21st century, Mexico is likely to continue to rely on trade with the USA to boost its economy. However, many Mexicans worry that their country may become little more than an economic satellite of the USA. Their fears seemed to be confirmed in 1995 when the USA intervened to prevent the collapse of the Mexican banks. The strict provisions of the intervention gave the USA virtual veto power over key elements of the Mexican economy.

For its part, the USA remains concerned about the large numbers of illegal immigrants who cross the border each year to supply the cheap labour that US agriculture demands. Many immigrants work for low pay in poor conditions. Concern also continues about Mexico's role in the traffic of illegal drugs from South and Central America to feed the huge demand in the USA.

are now more resorts and better facilities for visitors than ever before. In the 21st century, tourism should continue to flourish and expand.

In general, however, Mexico faces a troubled economic future. Inflation remains very high (about 9.5 per cent in 2000), but economic growth is slow. The country's economic difficulties look likely to continue well into the 21st century.

## Debt and dependence

The problems date back to the 1970s, when Mexico borrowed large sums to develop its oil industry. Now the country must try to pay off its debt or at least keep pace with the interest that is due on the borrowed money. Debts have continued to mount since 1995. In the late 1990s, the Mexican government managed to negotiate terms with its creditors that allowed the debts to be paid off more gradually.

In the 21st century, Mexico hopes to reap the benefits of the North American Free Trade Agreement (NAFTA) with the USA and Canada. The agreement should enable it to trade with these countries without restrictions, and will allow US and Canadian companies to set up factories in Mexico.

Mexican companies will no longer be protected by high tariffs. Low rates of pay in Mexico will encourage more foreign companies to invest in the country by setting up offices and factories. Mexican workers, however, fear that NAFTA will lay them open to exploitation.

## POLITICAL ISSUES

At home, NAFTA has helped contribute to popular discontent. Unrest has continued in the state of Chiapas, where the Indian rebel movement, the Zapatista National Liberation Army (EZLN), is fighting for more rights and a fairer distribution of land.

Since the troubles began in 1994, there have been many clashes between government troops and the Zapatistas (see pages 69 and 70). In 1997, 45 Indians protesting in the town of Acteal were killed by gunmen said to be backed by the government. In 1998, 100,000 people marched in Mexico City to demand that government troops withdraw from the troubled state.

*Poverty is still a major problem that faces Mexico. Slums like this one in Mexico City are developing in the suburbs of many of the country's cities.*

## The fall of the PRI

Since the beginning of the 1990s, support for Mexico's ruling party, the Institutional Revolutionary Party (PRI), had been waning. Opposing parties such as the National Action Party (PAN) and the Party of Democratic Revolution (PRD) won a series of local, state elections. In 1997, the PRI lost its majority in the Chamber of Deputies for the first time in nearly 70 years. Then, in 2000, PAN's leader, Vincente Fox, was elected as president, breaking the PRI's 71-year hold on the presidency. President Fox promised to reform Mexico's politics and end the corruption of the past. Today, however, some Mexicans feel that the pace of change is not fast enough.

## PROJECTED FUTURE POPULATION

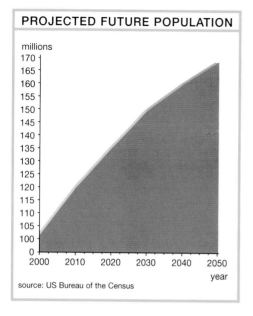

millions

source: US Bureau of the Census

*Experts predict that the population of Mexico will continue to grow massively over the coming decades. However, as living standards improve and social attitudes to issues such as contraception and abortion become more liberal, the rate of growth will slow. Nevertheless, in 2050, Mexico's population will be a huge 167 million.*

## CROWDED CITIES

During the late 1990s, Mexico's population continued to rise quickly. With about 38 per cent of the population under fifteen, this trend will only continue. Unemployment, already a problem in the 1980s, has been made worse by the population increase. Each year, many young people start to look for work, but few people retire from the job market.

People continue to move from country areas to the major cities, swelling the large numbers crowded in poor shanty towns. With a population of 18 million in 2000, Mexico City is considered to be the fastest-growing city in the world, but other major towns such as Guadalajara and Monterrey are also expanding quickly. In every decade since the 1960s, the population of the town of Tijuana, close to the US border, has doubled. Housing, health care and social services in urban areas struggle to keep pace. In the slums, polluted water and overcrowding are major problems.

At the beginning of the 21st century, the gap between the rich and poor in Mexico is widening. Mexico must continue to help its poorest people, both in towns and in the countryside. The government faces tough choices if it is to provide a better future for the young and ensure that the country's wealth is divided more equally.

## ENVIRONMENTAL ISSUES

In recent years, pollution has become a big issue in Mexico's largest towns. City air is polluted by fumes from factories in the suburbs and by vehicle exhausts. In Mexico City, the many millions of cars on the streets each day mean huge traffic jams as well as serious pollution. A pall of smog hangs over the city on most days, obscuring the mountains, and the capital is no longer a place 'where the air is clear' (see page 98). Eye diseases and breathing problems are becoming common, particularly among children.

Recently, Mexico's government has taken steps to improve the situation. Vehicles with certain registration numbers are banned from using city streets on one day a week. In the future, governments will need to take these measures much further by improving public transportation and tightening pollution controls.

### Threats to the landscape

Pollution is less of a problem in the countryside. Native plants and animals thrive in the vast areas of wild, empty country in Mexico, where few people live and no industry exists. However, in the tropical rainforests of the south and east, local wildlife is threatened as the forests are logged for timber or fuel, or cleared for ranching. Some areas have now been protected as nature reserves or national parks.

In the early 1990s, Mexico and four neighbouring countries – Belize, Guatemala, Honduras and El Salvador – came up with a clever way of protecting wildlife and boosting tourism at the same time. The **Mayan** Road is a route linking the principal ancient Mayan cities found in all five countries. This project, launched in 1993, attracts tourists to the ancient Mayan cities and brings much-needed cash to local people. In this way, the native Indians have a vested interest in protecting their environment.

*Several times a year, the pollution in Mexico City becomes so bad that the city government has to put roadblocks up to reduce vehicle use in the capital.*

# Almanac

## POLITICAL

**country name:**
official form: United Mexican States
short form: Mexico
local official form: *Estados Unidos Mexicanos*
local short form: *La Republica*

**nationality:**
noun: Mexican
adjective: Mexican

**official language:** Spanish

**capital city:** Mexico City (México)

**type of government:** federal republic

**suffrage (voting rights):** everyone eighteen years and over

**overseas territories:** none

**national anthem:** 'Mexicans at the Cry of War'

**national day:** 16 September (Independence Day)

**flag:**

## GEOGRAPHICAL

**location:** North America; latitudes 14.5° to 33° north and longitudes 88° to 117° west

**climate:** plateaux and high mountains are mostly warm; the south-east Pacific coast has a subtropical climate.

**total area:** 1,972,500 sq km (761,400 sq miles)
land: 97.5%
water: 2.5%

**coastline:** 9330 km (5830 miles)

**terrain:** high, rugged mountains, low coastal plains, high plateaux and desert

**highest point:** Mount Orizaba, 5700 m (18,696 ft)
**lowest point:** Lake Salada, 10 m (33 ft)

**natural resources:** zinc, petroleum, silver, copper, gold, lead, natural gas and timber

**land use:**
arable land: 12%

forests and woodland: 26%

permanent pasture: 39%

permanent crops: 1%

other: 22%

**natural hazards:** tsunamis (Pacific coast); volcanoes and earthquakes (centre and south)

## POPULATION

**population** (2002 est.): 103.4 million

**population growth rate** (2002 est.): 1.47%

**birth rate** (2002 est.): 22.4 births per 1000 of the population

**death rate** (2002 est.): 4.9 deaths per 1000 of the population

**sex ratio** (2002 est.): 97 males per 100 females

**fertility rate** (2002 est.): 2.6 children born for every woman in the population

**infant mortality rate** (2002 est.): 24.5 deaths per 1000 live births

**life expectancy at birth** (2002 est.):

total population: 73.4 years

male: 70.4 years

female: 76.4 years

**literacy** (2000):

total population: 90.1%

male: 92%

female: 87.7%

## ECONOMY

**currency:** Mexican new peso (N$); 1N$ = 100 centavos (¢)

**exchange rate** (2003): £1 = 17.75N$

**gross national product (GNP)** (1999): £302,500 million (eleventh-largest economy in the world)

**average annual growth rate** (1990–99): 2.7%

**GNP per capita** (1999): £3106

**average annual inflation rate** (1990–2000): 18.4%

**unemployment rate** (2001): 3%

**exports** (2001): £99,375 million

**imports** (2001): £105,000 million

**foreign aid received** (1995): £728 million

**Human Development Index**

(an index scaled from 0 to 100 combining statistics indicating adult literacy, years of schooling, life expectancy and income levels):

78.4 (UK 91.8)

# TIMELINE – MEXICO

**World history**

**Mexican history**

## c.20,000 BC

**c.14,000** Birth of El-Kebareh civilization in Israel

**c.20,000** First evidence of humans in central Mexico

## c.1500 BC

**c.2500** Ancient Egyptians build the pyramids in Giza

**c.1500** The Olmec build pyramids in Mexico's Gulf Coast region

## c.AD 300

**306** Constantine becomes Roman emperor and legalizes Christianity

**800** Charlemagne, king of the Franks, is crowned first Holy Roman emperor

The city of Teotihuacán dominates central Mexico. Its inhabitants build the huge Pyramid of the Sun.

The civilization of the Maya people flourishes in the Yucatán. The Maya invent a counting system, calendar and a script for writing.

**1520** The pope excommunicates (expels) Martin Luther from the Roman Catholic Church

**1492** Columbus arrives in America – Europe begins period of exploration and colonization

**1456** Gutenberg prints the first book in Europe

**1453** Constantinople falls to the Turks

**1348** The Black Death breaks out in Europe

**1200** The Incas build the city of Cuzco in Peru

**900** The Vikings land in North America

**1521** Tenochtitlán falls to the Spanish, and Mexico becomes part of the Spanish empire. The Spanish destroy many ancient towns and cities and convert natives to Roman Catholicism.

**1519** Hernán Cortés lands on the Gulf Coast

## c.1500

**1345** The Aztecs – a Mexican people – found Tenochtitlán. They establish an empire throughout central Mexico.

Mexica people arrive from the north and found rival cities in the Valley of México

## c.1300

The war-like Toltec migrate from northern Mexico and conquer much of central Mexico. Their capital, Tula, flourishes.

## c.900

**c.1600**

**1642–51** The English Civil War

**1700** The Bourbon dynasty of kings begins its rule over Spain. They reorganize Spain's colonies in South America.

***c.1750*** Industrial Revolution begins in England

Spanish immigrants come to New Spain and build new, European-style cities, including Mexico City and Puebla. Native peoples work under appalling conditions in silver mines and haciendas.

**2000** The West celebrates the Millennium – 2000 years since the birth of Christ

**1994** End of apartheid in South Africa

**2000** President Fox is elected, ending 71 years of PRI rule

**1994** The North American Free Trade Agreement (NAFTA) comes into effect

**c.1990**

**c.1800**

***c.1800*** Spain is in decline as a world power

**1810–24** Spanish colonies in mainland South America win independence

**1815** Napoleon is defeated at Waterloo

**1848** Famine leads to unrest and revolutions throughout Europe

**1810** The priest Miguel Hidalgo calls for Mexican independence from Spain (the Grito de Delores)

**1821** Mexico wins independence

**1836** The Mexican territory of Texas declares its independence from Mexico; the battles of the Alamo and San Jacinto follow

**1847** The USA occupies Mexico City; Mexico loses half of its territory

**1989** Fall of communism in eastern Europe

**1939–45** World War Two

**1914–18** World War One

**1985** Earthquake in Mexico City kills 7000

**1938** President Lázaros Cárdenas nationalizes the oil industry

**c.1900**

**1880s** European 'scramble for Africa'

***c.1870*** The USA overtakes Britain as largest world economy

**1851** France falls under the rule of Napoleon

**1876** The dictatorship of General Porfirio Díaz begins

**1867** Benito Juárez defeats Maximilian, and the emperor is executed

**1863** France invades Mexico. The Mexican army defeats the French at Puebla.

**c.1850**

# Glossary

**Abbreviations:**
Sp. = Spanish
Mex. Sp. = Mexican Spanish

**agave** member of a family of tall, spiny-leaved flowering plants

*alameda* (**Sp.**) city park

**Aztecs** Nahuatl-speaking people who dominated central Mexico at the time of the Spanish conquest

*azulejo* (**Sp.**) glazed, coloured tile, usually blue and white

*barranca* (**Sp.**) deep, steep-sided gully

**Calendar Round** ancient Mesoamerican 52-year cycle

**capital goods** raw materials that are imported or exported to produce other goods – for example, the steel needed to produce a car

*cenote* (**Sp.**) natural well found in the Yucatán

*chacmool* (**Mayan**) reclining stone figure found in ancient Mayan temples

*charreada* (**Sp.**) rodeo

*charro* (**Sp.**) cowboy

*chiampa* (**Sp.**) artificial field created on a framework of mud and reeds

*china poblana* (**Sp.**) Mexico's national costume for women

*ciudad perdida* (**Sp.** 'lost city') shanty town on the outskirts of Mexico City

**consumer goods** manufactured goods ready for sale directly to the public – for example, cars and clothes

*cordillera* (**Sp.**) system of mountain ranges

*criollo* (**Sp.**) someone of Spanish blood born outside Spain; creole

*dedazo* (**Sp.** 'touching with the finger')  president's practice of choosing his successor

*encomienda* (**Sp.**) tribute paid by Indians to their Spanish conquerors in the form of work

*ejido* (**Sp.**) communal farm

**exports** goods sold by one country to another

**foreign debt** money owed by a country to other countries

**gross national product** (**GNP**) total value of goods and services produced by the people of a country during a period, usually a year

*hacienda* (**Sp.**) large agricultural estate

**henequen** fibre obtained from a kind of agave and used to make rope or twine

**imports** goods bought by one country from another

*indígenas* (**Sp.**) Indians – the native people of Mexico

**inflation** annual rate at which prices increase

**intermediate goods** processed materials to be used for manufacturing other products – for example, the nuts and bolts for a car

**jai alai** Basque ball game with two or four players; also called *frontón*

*la Línea* (**Sp.** 'the line') Mexico's border with the USA

**literacy** as defined by UNESCO, the ability to read and write a simple sentence

**maguey** (**Sp.**) kind of agave, the sap of which is used to make the drink tequila

*maquiladoras* (**Sp.**) assembly plants in Mexico near the US border

*mariachi* (**Mex. Sp.**) Mexican strolling street musicians and their music

**Maya** Indian people of Honduras, Guatemala and south-eastern Mexico

**Mesoamerica** area of Central and North America occupied in ancient times by advanced cultures such as the Olmecs, Maya and Aztecs

*mestizo* (**Sp.** 'mixed') a person with both Spanish and Indian ancestry

*Mexica* (**Nahuatl**) general name by which the Aztecs called themselves

**Nahuatl** ancient language of the Aztecs that is still spoken widely today

124

*norteño* (**Sp.** 'northern') style of cooking or music in the north of Mexico

**Olmecs** ancient people of the Gulf Coast of Mexico who developed the first great civilization of Mesoamerica

*paseo* (**Sp.**) broad avenue

*peninsular* (**Sp.** 'from the [Spanish] peninsula') white, Spanish-born inhabitant of Latin America

*peón* (**Sp.**) bonded labourer

*pesero* (**Sp.**) shared taxi

*posada* (**Sp.**) festive procession

*pulque* (**Mex. Sp.**) alcoholic drink made from the fermented juice of the agave

*quetzal* (**Mex. Sp.**) tropical bird found in Mexico in the Chiapas Highlands

*saguaro* (**Mex. Sp.**) giant cactus

*techichi* (**Mex. Sp.**) barkless dog kept by the ancient Toltecs

*tezontle* volcanic rock used in Mexican buildings

**Toltecs** ancient people who dominated central Mexico before the Aztecs

*trajinera* (**Sp.**) gondola-style boat

*zócalo* (**Sp.**) main square in a town or city

# Bibliography

**Major sources used for this book**
Collis, John, and David Jones, *Mexico*. Blue Guides (W. W. Norton, 1997)
Lustig, Nora, *Mexico: The Remaking of an Economy* (Brookings Institute, 1998)
Meyer, Michael C., *The Course of Mexican History* (OUP, 1998)
Miller, Mary Ellen, *The Art of Mesoamerica (*Thames and Hudson, 1986)
Thomas, Hugh, *Montezuma, Cortes, and the Fall of Old Mexico* (Touchstone Books, 1995)

**General further reading**
Cootes, R. J., and L .E. Snellgrove, *The Ancient World* (Longman, 1991)
*The DK Geography of the World* (Dorling Kindersley, 1996)
*The Kingfisher History Encyclopedia.* (Kingfisher, 1999)
Martell, Hazel Mary, *The Kingfisher Book of the Ancient World* (Kingfisher, 1995)
*Student Atlas* (Dorling Kindersley, 1998)

**Further reading about Mexico**
Berdan, Frances F., *The Aztecs* (Chelsea House Publishing, 1993)
Bierhorst, John, *The Mythology of Mexico and Central America* (OUP, 1990)
Leone, Bruno, *The Mexican War of Independence* (Lucent Books, 1997)
O'Brien, Steven, *Pancho Villa*. Hispanics of Achievement series (Chelsea House, 1994)
Sayer, Chloe, *Arts and Crafts in Mexico* (Thames and Hudson, 1990)

**Some websites about Mexico**
Mexican Embassy in the UK
*www.embamex.co.uk*
Mexico for Kids
*www.elbalero.gob.mx/index_kids.html*

# Index

# Acknowledgements

**Cover photo credit**
Corbis: James A. Sugar

**Photo credits**
AKG London: 56; DACS, London 1999 96; Erich
Lessing 44; **Corbis:** Burstein Collection 62; Sergio
Dorantes 117; George Huey 12; Danny Lehman
111; Buddy Mays 91; Stephanie Maze 119; Phil
Schermeister 73; **ET Archive:** 52; **Hutchison Library:**
79; Robert Francis 22; Edward Parker 16, 33, 35, 41;
J. Pate 47; Liba Taylor 81, 101, 113; Isabella Tree 82;
**Image Bank:** Gabriel Covian 28, 77; Eric Meola 95;

Guido A. Rossi 6, 86; **Mexicolore:** 14, 43, 46, 54,
78, 108; Sean Sprague 98, 104; **Peter Newark's
American Pictures:** 60, 66; **NHPA:** Martin Harvey
27; Daniel Heuclin 24; B. Jones & M. Shimlock 26;
Dr Eckart Pott 25; Karl Switak 20; **South American
Pictures:** Robert Francis 36; Charlotte Lipson 106;
Pedro Martinez 64, 65; Tony Morrison 18, 32, 37,
70; Chris Sharp 58, 99; **Tony Stone Images:** Cosmo
Condina 92; Robert Frerck 30, 50; Mark Lewis 114;
Andy Sacks 74